adhyatmikta

Explorations into Hindu Spiritual Practices

adhyatmikta

Explorations in Hindu Spiritual Traditions

adhyatmikta

Explorations into Hindu Spiritual Practices

Rajarshi Ranjan Nandy

Title: Adhyatmikta: Explorations into Hindu Spiritual Practices
Author: Rajarshi Ranjan Nandy

ISBN: 978-93-92209-40-6

First published in India 2023
This edition published 2023

Published by:
BluOne Ink LLP
306, Tower-I, Assotech Business Cresterra,
Plot No. 22, Sector 135, Noida.

Website: www.bluone.ink
Email: publisher@bluone.ink

Printed at Nutech Print Services, India.

Kali, Occam and BluPrint are all trademarks of BluOne Ink LLP.

Contents

꩜

PART II

Beginning

>᷒᷒᷒ᕏᖤᕏ᷒᷒᷒<

I had begun my exploration into Hindu spirituality in 2005, right after Durga Puja. It was a challenging time as I battled with troubles on multiple fronts. I had no clear solution in sight until a chance encounter with a *tantropasaka*, whom I regard as one of my gurus—he turned things around and gave me a glimpse of a world different from what the five senses and the rational mind can comprehend. It also landed me on a path of sadhana, and I started to explore for myself if there was any truth to it.

In fact, days before that eventful meeting, I had the first conscious and concrete experience that defied all logic. I was inside a *pandal* in Bengaluru and as it happens in Durga Puja, there was a typical ambience of chatty socializing amid a festive mood. I was looking around, observing people, their activities and the decorations of the idol and comparing it in my mind with other idols in other pandals, when suddenly, it felt as if all noise around me had been cut off, and I was inside a zone of absolute silence. I could see before my eyes not just a *vigraha* but a pair of living eyes—a powerful, undeniable presence. It was right after this that I met my first guru within a week, who gave me a mantra *upadesam*. Thereafter I started a routine of daily mantra *japa*, which carried on unbroken for a year, until again during the next Durga Puja I had another strange experience, which was not only beyond any rational logic but also quite unnerving, at least temporarily.

In April 2007, after coming back from an unplanned Kumbh Mela trip, I started practising *homas* as a *sadhana*, which continued for many years. From 2007 till today, as I write this, the fire has remained a constant in my sadhana, though the understanding and engagement with this powerful medium underwent drastic shift over time. When used in the right manner and in the right proportion it becomes a very useful source of mantric application. However, indiscriminate use can lead to problems.

That one trigger in 2005 led to a long journey of sadhana that went on parallel to regular life. I explored, evolved, practised, met advanced *upasakas* and *sadhakas*, visited many ancient *kshetras* and *pithas* reputed to have special spiritual potency, gathered deeper experience in sadhana, analyzing my own understanding of these matters in the light of new evidence. I often took U-turns as needed, deconstructed my assumptions until eventually I could, with greater experience, settle into a personalized understanding of sadhana and *adhyatma*. A landmark stage in my own development was the discovery of Sri Aurobindo and the Mother's writings. Another one was Ramana Maharishi and the mystical power of Arunachala. Throughout this book you will find references from the lives and words of famous saints, especially Ramana Maharishi, Sri Aurobindo and Ramakrishna Paramahamsa, when explaining some spiritual aspect. While the wisdom of these masters remains an undeniable influence, my own path finally settled in the *tantropasana* of the *mahapitha* of Kamakhya.

Though I had self-published this book earlier, I have added some new sections in this edition of the book. This is not a book meant to act as a primer on Hinduism or the more accurate term, Sanatana Dharma. It is not for those who believe in the calendar-art version of pop-Hinduism that amusingly normalizes Dharma into banal quotable quotes. Neither is it aimed to warm the cockles of the orthodox hearts, or the literalists, or self-appointed guardians of any specific path. Only a non-sectarian, sincere sadhaka of Sanatana Dharma, whose inner attachment to the deity surpasses his attachment to any specific sampradaya, and who is keen to experience the gods for the joy and richness that such an experience can bring may find this book useful, not in the sense of a final or definitive text of adhyatma, but more as an exercise in honest exploration of the spiritual path and process involved, with as much objectivity as one may subjectively muster.

The first half of this book comprises a collection of thoughts and observations on different topics related to adhyatma, while the second half contains essays on some deities within Hinduism. Some of these essays have been published earlier in magazines and online forums.

PART I

Are Indians Naturally Spiritual?

Generally, Indians are brought up in an environment of religion-inspired culture and tradition right from childhood. As a Bengali proverb goes: *baro mashe tero parbon,* referring to the 13 festivals (of the religious kind) that fall in the 12 months of a year. Every year during festivals like Diwali, Eid (and a few others), which are celebrated all over India with great enthusiasm, we dress up in the best attires, exchange happy greetings, connect with friends and family, perform traditionally mandated rituals and prayers and generally spend a day in buoyant holiday spirit. That effectively sums up a religious holiday for an average Indian.

So, does it mean that Indians are naturally spiritual? Before we can answer that question, we need to understand what being spiritual means. Some believe that it refers to having certain kinds of predefined psychological experiences, or perceiving occult realities, or having access to 'supernatural' abilities, or possessing profound erudition in the scriptures and ritualistic traditions of one or more formal religions. The Bhagavad Gita, which is one of the most revered Indian religious texts, describes a dialogue between Krishna, the God who descended on Earth, and Arjuna, the warrior torn between righteous duty and love for his relatives, where they delve into this eternal question—how does one know a spiritual person? For it is, as we shall see, not through axiomatic statements but by analysis and observation of how these spiritual processes or states affect a person's worldview and engagement with life around him that the essential spirituality quotient of an individual can be judged.

In Chapter II of the Bhagavad Gita, Arjuna asks Krishna:

अर्जुन उवाच
स्थित प्रज्ञस्य का भाषा समाधिः तस्य केशव
स्थितधीः किं प्रभाषेतः किमासीत व्रजेत किम्

(What are the signs of one whose consciousness has been fixed and steady in Wisdom? In what manner does he speak, what kind of language does he use, how does he sit, how does he walk?)

In the next few verses Krishna explains the external signs of a spiritual man. Such a man is neither perturbed by sorrows of life nor is he exuberant in happiness. He remains unaffected by attachment, anger and fear. He can withdraw his sense organs from engaging in external objects as a tortoise withdraws its limbs inside the shell. His consciousness remains ever fixed on a greater transcendental reality. Such a one must be known as a great saint.

In other words, when a man truly takes a spiritual turn, it reflects to the world outside as a control over sensory indulgence, and a marked reduction from normal levels of reaction to external provocations. The same situations which would have elicited a strong response earlier, often involuntary, in the form of anger or hatred or lust or greed or possessiveness—any of the *sad-ripus* or six chains that bind the normal consciousness—would now evoke a reaction far less intense. And such a man will be able to detach himself from the vagaries of life, because he will perceive the basic impermanence of it all, and go about things, even those which are apparently unpleasant, with a tranquil mind and a steady heart. Without going into complex theological and spiritual analysis, these verses form the most fundamental parameters for judging a spiritual man. All rituals, all paths, all traditions are designed to finally inculcate this attitude towards life and death. It remains as the firm, unshakable basis on which the giant tree of spirituality must stand and bloom.

Now that we have some understanding of spirituality, let us return to our original question: are Indians more spiritual than people from other countries? Not really. On an average, we are just as good or as bad as any other race of people. Anyone living in India will know this. Underneath the mushrooming of market-friendly spiritual brands, the traditional as well as the new-age acts, or those who do a bit of both sides is a collective of spiritually untransformed human beings. The famed Indian Yogic stoicism, historically, in its mass manifestation has turned into a passive resignation to things which appear more powerful than us; our faith in the Divine is but a fragile caricature of past legacies, while our overall spirituality has become a skeleton of customary traditions to be followed, whose living spirit does not enthuse our shallow lives, notwithstanding the massive crowds that gather at professionally managed and widely televised 'satsangs' (holy gatherings), or the high-sounding ancient philosophies which we love to throw around during any discourse that touches on spirituality and religion, or the long list of religious holidays that mark a calendar year.

To the one who takes on this most difficult adventure of transformation, every day is a chance for self-improvement; every act an opportunity to observe and rectify all that is ignorant and opaque inside us. Everything can be turned into a festival of the Spirit.

Having said that, India does have a unique advantage over any other place in the world. The amount of spiritual exploration that has happened in this subcontinent for countless millennia, and the powerful energy that it has generated in the intellectual and vital atmosphere of this land, coupled with the wide range of fantastic paths and methodologies available, India can be a true goldmine for any sincere Seeker. Perhaps there is no essential path of spiritual transformation which has not been explored to its maximum depth in this land, including paths which preclude any belief in things supernatural to start off the spiritual journey. The collective pressure of all this makes Indians as a race certainly more pliant and open to genuine, experiential spirituality. That may also be the reason why there have been such endless streams of Reality-addicted, for that is what it finally is, a study of unconditioned Reality—men and women who have lived across the length and breadth of this subcontinent from a very ancient time.

A good saint once remarked that at any given point, only a handful will experience and live the life of the Spirit, while the rest will remain happy scratching the surface. That is how nature plays the game. This may well be true. While essential spirituality will always remain a 'flight of the alone to the alone', as Plotinus so poignantly observed, living in India can potentially help in opening the average mind and life to that elusive touch of the infinite than other places.

The Path

Spirituality has many different paths that one may follow depending on the attitude, temperament and *purva samskaras* of the *sadhaka*. Sometimes one may have to travel a long, circuitous route before he can find what suits him best. Once the exact sadhana, the correct path, the right deity, the most appropriate mantra is found, the journey of the Seeker becomes much smooth and easy.

Raja yogic meditation, pranayama-based *kriyas*, or *upasana* of deities—all of these work extremely well with the right kind of Seeker. Such a wide variety offers different individuals with different tendencies the choice to pick what works best for them. Besides, there are different Divine forms as enunicated by rishis— some gentle, some fierce, but all of them are extremely capable of helping a sincere sadhaka to progress on that path. Sometimes a devata may have multiple forms, where each form captures the spiritual reality of that God. None of these are random artistic imaginations but carefully selected images representing various aspects of the energy manifested by that devata.

What is of vital importance, therefore, is to choose not only the right devata, but also the right form of the devata which will suit one's temperament and attitude—that is the path to the fastest spiritual growth.

Leaving aside a minor fraction of great souls born with exceptional purva samskaras, making this judgment about the shortest path to spirituality is near impossible for most people.

This is where the Guru becomes most important, for it is the role of the Guru to guide one in their spiritual journey, and offer the Guru-mantra, which helps the Seeker connect with the stream of the Guru's consciousness. Hence, it is rightly assumed that it is the Guru who has the Divine ability to see which is the right spiritual path for an individual. This cannot be done merely by mental calculations or quick thinking or rehashing what one has read in books, but only by actually traversing the path and accomplishing the results by oneself. Thus, in short, a Guru is one who has obtained *siddhi* of the path and therefore knows who is the best fit for which route of sadhana—a knowledge acquired not only by experience but also by a supranormal connection with the Divine.

Preliminary Sadhana

As is commonplace today, people have a desire for spirituality but no guidance on how to set out on the spiritual path. Some believe that they must wait for the opportune moment when the Guru comes and guides them; this is a good idea but a slow one for sure. The other school of thought is to start with sadhana anyway and keep walking in good faith and sincerity so that the force of previous samskaras will drive the journey into the proper channels while creating a new conducive momentum of karmas, which will certainly help the Seeker.

One can start with any deity, pick a general mantra and chant at least a few *malas*. Sadhana only works if done with consistency of mind, body and spirit in disciplined fashion with concentration and time devoted to the practice. A five-minute daily namaskara in the puja room at home is least likely to precipitate a strong effect on an individual, whereas doing at least an hour, preferably two, of meditation or mantras, even generic ones, while maintaining discipline in food, sleep, speech, and timing of sadhana increases the likelihood of powerful spiritual experiences coming to the Seeker.

If not mantras, one can also pick a *stotra* of a deity that appeals to the sadhaka, or a standard spiritual text like an Upanishad or the Gita and meditate on a line or paragraph from it. But one must spend at least an an hour every day for a few months before the results may show. The initial stages of sadhana can often bring very quick and solid results—and then it hits a plateau, which can appear endless. Crossing this plateau of no-results is where many seekers drop out from the path. There is no easy solution for this except to keep walking in good faith, till the inevitable and eventual victory of sadhana becomes a living reality. Patience is the armour that never fails a sadhaka.

Meditation

One of the best practices of sadhana in this age is to develop the habit of meditating in silence. Sit in a comfortable posture, *sukhasana*, or in the lotus posture, *padmasana*, and then focus the mind either in the centre of the eyebrows or in the heart. There are other places one may focus on, but these two are universally regarded as the best. One may try the method of *atma-vichara*, meditating on the question: Who am I?, as the great sage of Arunachala, Ramana Maharishi, would advise people to do. The most important factor, however, is to practise sitting still for an hour or more, with zero body movements. If one does not succeed in a day, keep trying until it is achieved. If one cannot sit on the floor, then use a chair, or any comfortable seat, but remain physically immobile. Once the body is taught to remain perfectly steady and still, with not even the slightest movements, then the breathing eventually becomes calm, and finally, the mind is forced to reduce its fluctuations and become more concentrated and quieter. Eventually, the mind becomes so controlled that one can continue to be in a meditative state even when engaged in any other activity. That is a significant advancement in sadhana.

Even *mantra japa* works better if the sadhaka improves their capacity for meditation. As the Seeker keeps chanting a mantra, eventually the mind will use the power of the mantra to enter into a meditative zone, where the mantra becomes one with the individual's inner being and then the sacred words start to effect one, first internally, and then externally. In that excellent state, uttering the mantra even a few times will take much longer than usual, because the concentration becomes extremely acute and sharp. Meditation is undoubtedly the royal road to the Divine.

Rituals, Reforms, Orthodoxy, Orthopraxy

Rituals are the heart of any religious-cultural system, especially one that is polytheistic. It is a language of communication between the human realm and the spiritual worlds. It is for most parts non-negotiable and fixed by great rishis and masters who had the ability to make contact with these invisible realms. To ensure the sanctity of the process, strict fidelity to the ritual method is most important. Any frivolous tampering, regardless of the intention, can lead to loss of result or, in some cases, negative consequences. The settled knowledge of such orthopraxy over centuries, which has been coded in texts is known as *sadhana dharma* or *sadhana shatras*. They are non-negotiable, designed by the great spiritual geniuses of the race where all worst case scenarios have been taken into account while formulating the rules. Therefore, they provide protection when systematically followed, which no human being can provide—howsoever smart and intelligent—certainly not the new-age kinds whose depth and realization itself is a big question mark. It is strict adherence to orthopraxy alone that allowed the sound of the Vedas to survive to this day in the specific *swara* and *chhanda*. This is why verses and chanting continues to be done in the exact meter and tone for centuries by those who have carried forward the Vedic traditions. Without their superhuman fidelity to orthopraxy, the Vedas may not have reached us today.

Then there is the cultural and societal aspect of customary Dharma. This is orthodoxy. This keeps changing from time to time based on various currents and movements. In fact, even at the peak of Hindu civilization one cannot say that everyone adhered to the perfect orthodoxy. Instead, an idealized set of *niyamas* were followed at a particular time and context.

It is orthodoxy that requires reform in Dharma. On the contrary, the concept of orthopraxy has never needed to be reformed, since it is based on being righteous in one's conduct and not just religious. In fact, whenever someone has tried tampering with orthopraxy, even if intially such a *sampraday* or institution looked promising, eventually it has perished, since such institutions have zero innate power. This is especially true of the colonial rule, when many new non-ritualistic Hindu samajist organizations came up, they started with a lot of zeal and strength, only to fizzle out in time. On the other hand, the Ramakrishna Mutt, which otherwise maintains strict fidelity to orthopraxy, is very particular about how they perform the Durga and Kali puja—every ritual is carried out as per the shastras. It is because of Swami Vivekananda, whose brilliant foresight knew where the heart of Dharma lay that orthopraxy remained unchanged in the ritual space. It explains why they continue to remain a vibrant organization even a century later, while many others have collapsed and lost relevance. Fidelity to rituals in a polytheistic system is key to developing Shakti. This is how every single *sampradaya*, even though old, has continued to thrive for centuries.

Besides, who can reform orthopraxy? Almost no one can—as simple as that. Religious texts offer a wide range of options for *sadhana*, depending on the capacity and competency of an individual. One can choose which is suitable and appropriate and take up that practice. Never bite more than one can chew and under no circumstance delude oneself into thinking one has to perform the most complex ritual engagement but with zero commitment of rules, time, sacrifice—some further delude oneself into believing this is service to Dharma. It is just service to one's ego and brings a sense of entitlement at best. Besides, one cannot set out on the path of reforming a religious practice without an in-depth understanding of its birth and growth. Take for instance the most famous social reformer, Raja Rammohan Roy, who studied Vedanta under a traditional pandit in Kashi for 12 years, then took *tantra diksha* from a respected *acharya* in Bengal, then studied the *Mahanirvana Tantra* and other texts, and then went about doing what he was doing. Thus, it is critical to study and assimilate a tradition well and only then think of questioning or changing it, if at all. And that too mostly in the orthodoxy aspect, never in orthopraxy. How many of those whose agenda seems to be reform have undergone even a fraction of the training that Rammohan Roy underwent, or read the shastric debates between Vidyasagar and the pundits of Varanasi?

It would not be wrong to say that given the circumstances and environment today, the word 'reform' remains deeply suspicious. In its present usage, it hides a sense of entitlement and reflects a lack of understanding or acknowledgment of *adhikara*, *niyama* or other *angas*. It is a bit like saying, I want to drive a car, but I refuse to get a license. Considering the forces at play, Hindus would be better served to stick more diligently to orthopraxy. That is the only saviour of Dharma in the future.

Dharma and Adhyatma

‿︵✦︵‿

Our ancients perceived human life to be guided by four primary motivations: Dharma, *artha*, *kama*, and *moksha*. Where Dharma dictates the rightly guided conduct in every walk of life, artha is often translated to mean financial power or money, kama refers to desires, and finally, moksha is liberation. Even the pursuit of artha and kama must be regulated by Dharma for it to help an individual in a large enough timescale. Dharma, therefore, is vital—it is one of the key fundamental concepts in Hinduism. Various texts have defined Dharma in different ways but observing the general trend of thought over time and the way in which great saints have used this term, Dharma is largely that which is guided by a sense of natural truthfulness in a sphere in a specific *desh-kaal-patra*. Dharma encompasses various practices—from conducting appropriate rituals on different occasions to behaving in a manner that befits a situation. An individual is faced with several kinds of Dharma in their lifetime—Dharma to one's parents, one's spouse, to children, relatives, friends, society, nation, heritage, culture, etc. The Gita, therefore, uses the term *swadharma*—one's own Dharma—and indicates that it is based on the *gunas* or tendencies within an individual. It is better to follow one's swadharma and die than to follow someone else's swadharma. Dharma cannot be copied.

Swadharma, however, is the beginning of the journey. As one follows it diligently and at the same time tries to spiritually transform one's consciousness by following a conscious yogic regime, their swadharma will also change. As the inner perspectives change, so does the Dharma that one is driven to follow. This is common knowledge and intuitively correct. Finally, when one makes an entry into the spiritual zones, most of our preconceived notions about Dharma must be left behind. The Gita attests to this universal fact when Krishna urges Arjuna to drop all Dharmas and 'come to Me, I will deliver you from sin'. This idea is reiterated by other forms of Indian spiritual literature, for the Divine is beyond every duality of the mind. To reach there one must outgrow all ideas, imaginations, and preconceptions. This is why our sages perceived Dharma and moksha as two different motivations that guide human existence.

There is another way to understand this. Dharma evolves as the consciousness of the individual becomes deeper, expansive and more subtle. Eventually, from swadharma the *sadhaka* will enter into eternal Dharma, or Sanatana Dharma. But for that to happen, one must first get into real contact with something truly unchanging and eternal, and there is nothing which fits that description except for the Divine. In the Mahabharata everyone had their own understanding of Dharma—some thought of it as loyalty to family, friends, their kingdom, unbreakable vows, etc., but it was only

Krishna whose perspective was truly eternal, Sanatana. Hence, it is his words in the Gita that are treated as timeless precepts for all genuine seekers of Truth, not the ruminations of various other characters howsoever learned or powerful they might have been during their lifetime.

Ego

All streams of spirituality finally enter the highest spiritual realms only when the ego is permanently annihilated. The word ego is not to be understood in the typical sense of pride, which is one manifestation of it, but rather as the I-sense within an individual. Forced humility is as much a sign of ego as is bashful pride. In fact, this I-sense is what makes each one a functioning human being, with a distinct personality. It runs like a psychological thread tying the five sheaths or *koshas* that make up an individual and helps to maintain a sense of distinctiveness, that innate feeling of being different from others and the world around.

The true spiritual process is designed to take a sadhaka beyond the human condition, into something Divine, and remake himself in the image of devata. For this, the most fundamental obstacle is the I-sense. Whatever path of sadhana one may adopt, the final shift in consciousness never comes until this I-sense is finished off permanently. With that done all the major obstacles of sadhana like the six *ripus* or chains that bind the consciousness are broken for good. And once this I-sense is destroyed, the sadhaka is then governed entirely by the Self—the *atma* or the deity one worships. Thus, the two—the worshipper and the worshipped effectively become one.

All great experiences are possible when the ego has been transcended. Finally, someday every sadhaka will be able to do it, except that it may take several lifetimes of effort to reach it for there is no greater trickster than the human ego in this world. It is hard to kill it, and it remains immune to any mental rationalizing because it is subtler and far more powerful than the mind. We are our ego, and this is the self as we know it. Since we do not really vanish when we die, our self too does not vanish entirely after physical death, except for severing the connection between the body and the higher koshas.

The ego is also a master at creating massive illusions of all kinds while ensuring its own survival. It can lawyer excellent arguments with one express aim to justify its existence. Destroying the ego is the one-stop spiritual solution for all problems, and yet it remains the toughest job because the I-sense displays a greater tenacity for survival than perhaps even cockroaches surviving a nuclear blast! The great Milarepa, arguably the most legendary yogi of Tibet said, 'My religion is not deceiving myself'. Especially for all who are in sincere pursuit of the eternal atma, this is the best advice to remember.

Satguru

Regard only Him who possesses the rare attribute of radiating that Supreme Power as the Satguru (Great Master) who has the enormous power to merge, through his causeless sweet Grace, any individual self that comes to Him with genuine love into the non-duality of the Absolute Supreme, whose nature is attribute-free consciousness.

-Ramana Maharishi

While religious texts mention different kinds of gurus that an individual may have, it is the Satguru among them all who is accorded the maximum importance, for it is only he who can guide a sadhaka who is ready in the truest sense to enter the highest spiritual consciousness, a state we call self-realization. Every other spiritual experience is easier than attaining realization of the Self.

Most religious traditions maintain that a Satguru is a must for the Seeker if he must enter into the highest state. This is by and large true for all practical purposes. However, the challenge lies in finding a Satguru and becoming a true disciple. Who is a Satguru? And why is he so important?

Ramana Maharishi compared the spiritual path to a mountain. The one who has reached the peak of that mountain can see everyone else who is climbing. Such a man can give valuable suggestions to those climbing up, even if that may not be the route through which they had climbed. This is the best analogy of a Satguru—someone who has reached the peak of the metaphorical mountain of *adhyatma*, that every genuine Seeker is trying to climb. To understand what makes a genuine Satguru different from an ordinary *upasaka*, one must understand the nature of the mind very clearly.

The human mind works in the best-case scenario, by the process of friction, adding logic upon logic in bits and pieces until it reaches a solution or synthesis. But, more often than not, it is governed by emotions either consciously or subconsciously. We are rational in name only; we are mostly emotional in our functioning. What does that mean? Our emotions make us choose an answer based on our own prejudices and biases, and then we use the rationalizing capacity of the mind to find a logic that supports our pre-formed conclusions. Since emotions are irrational, so are our judgments and resultant actions. At other times the mind either lives in the imagination of the past, or expectation of the future.

But a mind this unsettled, driven by irrationality is perfectly useless for higher spiritual transformation. At a certain stage of spiritual growth, an experience and realization come onto the Seeker which forces the mind to literally stop in its tracks, never to rise again. Let us call this the Silent Mind. There is no more a background story going on inside the head with the individual as the central character, which is normally what happens to all of us. The mind just drops like a veil and reveals something steady, deep, immediate and silent within us. Ramana Maharishi called this *manonasha*—destruction of the mind. No doubt this is very, very difficult to achieve. However, with long strenuous meditation and other *sadhanas* it is possible in moments of great exertion to curb the mind and reign it back from its usual meandering, but more often than not, it is merely temporary. The mind rises again in full force once the sadhana is over. Such temporary immobilization of the mind may cause interesting experiences for the Seeker, but it's rarely transformative or leaves a permanent change on the psychology of the sadhaka. So, the key point to be reached in this journey is to permanently centre the mind in stillness.

So how does such an individual whose mind has entered a higher condition behave and act? How does he decide, or make choices? In that state of Silent Mind, a Divine guidance comes in and directs every action of that individual. This is akin to actualizing the *charama shloka* of the Gita in a sadhaka's life:

सर्व धर्मान् परित्यज्य मामेकं शरणं व्रज
अहं त्वं सर्व पापेभ्यो मोक्षयिष्यामि मा शुचः

(Give up all dharma and take refuge in Me (Divine), I shall deliver you from all sins and lead you to Moksha.)

Such an individual does not do anything out of ego but instead, they are then truly and effectively an instrument in the hands of the Divine, *nimittamatra*, with no personal preference or judgement about any action they perform as prompted by the Divine. Whatever action is performed in this condition is most decisive, impactful and has far-reaching consequences. Only such an individual is fit to be a Satguru, for the guidance they provide comes from a direct flow of the Divine energy unhampered by the defects of their own mental or emotional instrumentation. And this state of transcending the normal mind is not the result of one specific path or sadhana, but a station which must be crossed irrespective of the path a sadhaka walks or the *sampradaya* they may belong to, like an important junction point through which all routes leading to the Divine must pass at some point or the other.

Whosoever has reached this station, gone beyond and effectively integrated that rare state along with carrying out their duties, where one is effectively guided by the Divine in some manner at all times of their existence, is a true Satguru and is fit to guide others. Anyone else who self-appropriates the title of a Satguru may provide some help and mentoring on and off but will fail to guide a Seeker in the long run, for such an individual has not yet reached the transformed state in his consciousness. One can only give to others what one has realized within, nothing more and nothing less.

Testing the Guru

It is critical today to test the Guru before accepting them as one's true guide. Quite often, there are people who may have had a spiritual experience or even developed some unusual abilities but not yet reached a transformed state of consciousness. They continue to operate from their ego-minds and believe they have become satgurus and great masters. This is nothing more than self-delusion and a belief arising from a place of ego. The word 'Satguru' carries a weight of its own and should not be diluted so easily. Only someone who is truly beyond the six chains that bind consciousness is a true Satguru. This is possible only when the central axis of the human mind, the I-sense or *aham*, has been destroyed completely and the individual is in constant contact with the Divine. Sri Aurobindo said that spirituality and character can only be taught through live examples, not by sermons. Therefore, it is but apt that someone desirous of being a disciple must test the Guru and be satisfied before unquestioningly accepting all advice from them.

Even Ramakrishna did not object when his disciples tested him before accepting his words as true. As is common knowledge, once some of his disciples placed some money under his bed. They wanted to test if Ramakrishna's claim that he was allergic to money was the truth or just holy pretense. To their utter shock, Ramakrishna, a nineteenth century devotee of Kali, found it impossible to sleep on the bed and complained of something disturbing as soon as he touched the bed. When he later learnt that he was being tested, he told his disciples that it was fair and proper to test a Guru. So, if someone of the calibre of Ramakrishna Paramhamsa could be tested, it stands to reason and common sense that much greater caution needs to be exercised in this age.

The *Kathamrita* records that Ramakrishna would recommend to his disciples that one must always observe a saint when he is in public and when he is in private, observe his words and his actions, and look for gaps in the same. Only spiritual talk does not mean much, for the world is not without great speakers who have no spirituality in them.

It is also good to remember that even in the age of the Mahabharata, at a time probably far less corrupted than ours, Lord Krishna forced Arjuna to fight against his gurus when the latter were seen to stand with *adharma*. Reverence and dedication to a genuine Satguru can propel a Seeker quickly on the path of spiritual growth, while one's association with someone unfit can as quickly pull them down. It is better not to a have a Guru than to have a wrong Guru, else one is likely to fall off the metaphorical mountain of spirituality.

Judging the Impact of a Spiritual Mentor

What exactly is a failsafe way to determine the spirituality of a saint? Consider the period one spends in interacting with a spiritual Guru/figure. What effect does it leave on your consciousness—has such an interaction heightened inner peace, silence, equanimity, inner strength or calm? At least one of these will increase over time if one is. On the other hand, if one finds oneself plunging more into chaos, confusion, anger and ego-driven disturbances, one must avoid the said individual like a plague, for there is likely to be nothing genuinely spiritual in such a person, or quite simply, such an individual has not yet reached a definitive state of consciousness from where they can guide others authentically.

Such a Guru or mentor is misaligned to the Seeker's spiritual goals. The blunt truth would be that such an individual is probably unfit to adorn the mantle of a genuine Guru.

This test cannot be done in one day but may take months or, a year or so, at least. However, it never fails. If the initial interaction increases agitation within, then avoid further mingling with such a 'spiritual' character.

It may be argued that there are certain gurus, particularly of the old schools, as stated in spiritual texts, whose first interaction with a devotee may cause a precipitation of great difficulties in the life of the Seeker, a sudden and violent acceleration of karmic repercussions. But after that phase of karmic cleaning is over, a greater and deeper stability and peace will reign inside the consciousness. A genuine transformation will be affected within, and this will create a new inner poise, and a sanguine strength, for after a stormy phase of karmic cleaning if there is no greater peace, calm and happy clarity, then the lessons are far from over. In any case, if one has interacted with a Guru/mentor for few years and finds only an increase of confusion and chaos, with no sign of the situation improving into a more positive state, know for certain there is something insufficient going on.

Non-Human Guru

Ramana Maharishi was often asked about the lack of a physical Guru in his life. To this he would unhesitatingly refer to the holy Arunachala Mountain as the Guru who caused his own spiritual transformation. Every genuine Seeker must have a Guru, whether human or non-human, depending on the nature of the sadhaka.

During his stay in Baroda, Sri Aurobindo was searching for someone who could guide him in his sadhana. His brother Barin had learnt of a Maharastrian Guru named Vishnu Bhaskar Lele, and promptly sent a telegram inviting him to Baroda. Lele later told A. B. Purani, who later became a disciple of Sri Aurobindo, that when he received the telegram he had an intuition that he would have to give initiation to a very great soul. Sri Aurobindo recollected that Lele asked him to observe his own mind and see how thoughts came from outside, and to reject them all. He wanted Sri Aurobindo to silence his mind and develop a relationship with the personal Godhead. He instructed that in the silence a voice would arise. What Sri Aurobindo instead experienced was an 'undefinable reality... beyond space and time'. He had entered a state of nirvana and remained in continuous meditation for seven days. Before leaving, Sri Aurobindo sought Lele's guidance, who offered detailed instructions on meditating at a fixed time daily.

Two months later Lele himself came to Calcutta to check on his disciple and asked him if he was following the instructions to meditate at a fixed time. Sri Aurobindo replied in the negative. Lele, who was furious on hearing this, claimed that if Sri Aurobindo neglected the instruction, he would be taken over by the 'devil'. Aurobindo replied in his characteristic style that he was ready to follow the 'devi' whereever it may lead him. By that time Sri Aurobindo had already been receiving guidance and instruction from his inner Guru. Besides, he was practically meditating throughout the day. That was the end of his interaction with Vishnu Bhaskar Lele.

After parting ways with Lele, Sri Aurobindo never had any human Guru and later, four of Lele's close disciples eventually left Lele and accepted the Saint of Pondicherry as their Guru. Sri

Aurobindo in time started receiving a Divine command, *adesha*, and guidance from Sri Krishna during his period of incarceration, which accelerated his sadhana and gave him many powerful experiences.

The first spiritual experience in the life of Ramakrishna Paramahamsa was the vision of Goddess Bhavatarini inside the Dakshineswar Temple. After this landmark event in his spiritual life, he met many gurus from the Tantrik Bhairavi Brahmai to the Adwaitic Totapuri. However, right at the beginning of his spiritual trajectory, even before a single guru manifested into his life, Ramakrishna once had a remarkable vision where he saw a subtle form of a yogi coming out of his own body and showing him the path that he would traverse, the different gurus he would have and various spiritual conditions he would experience, every one of which went on to be true later. Who was it that came out of Ramakrishna's body? In the light of this event, it may not be incorrect to say that his own inner guide was his primary Guru, the external gurus came later only to fulfill the prediction that had been made by his own Self.

What If There is No Guru?

It is a typical new age idea that one can manage entirely without a Guru. But that is, practically speaking, very unlikely, given the amount of karmic filth we carry with us. Oftentimes a true Satguru's dedication to transforming his disciple into a reflection of his own spiritual condition can be single-pointed and unnerving for those who are not yet ready for such a drastic transformation. Consider this anecdote by Nochur Venkataraman, a renowned spiritual leader from South India, in one of his talks.

A Guru of the Adwaitic persuasion in South India had a small thatched hut-like ashram, where he lived and was visited by his disciples. He would read the Upanishads with his disciples in the day, and then at night give each one a line from the text to meditate on, while he would sit and meditate with them, till such time the disciple had an experiential understanding of that statement. This was very important to him. Sometimes he would be awake with a disciple all night until he had an experience. One such disciple was, however, unable to meditate or experience any spiritual awakening even after the Guru worked with him exclusively for a few days. When the Guru asked him why he was unable to meditate, and what is it that was bothering him the disciple answered that the Guru had asked him to fix a part of the ashram a few days ago as monsoons were approaching. So, every time he would try to sit calmly and meditate, the thought of finishing that work came to his mind and he would not be able to concentrate. The Guru understood and did not make any further comment. That night he took the disciple to an abandoned Shiva temple in the outskirts of the town, again taught him to meditate and asked him to sit there and practice. The disciple did exactly as he was told but was still met with failure. Early morning, he came out of the temple and headed towards the ashram, only to find the whole thatched hut of the ashram burning furiously. His Guru was standing next to the hut with a fire torch in hand and said to him, 'I have burned down the ashram because nothing is so important that it must stand in the way of self-realization!' The disciple later went onto become a great *jnani* himself.

In the lives of a few great saints from the past era, we do not find evidence of the presence of a human Guru. David Godman, who is a leading authority on the life and times of Ramana Maharishi, notes that the Saivism of South India speaks of three types of seekers. Those in the first and biggest category need a human Guru because they have massive impurities or spiritual impediments. The second category comprises devotees who are extremely pure. These people can realize the Self by having a devata appear to them as a Guru, who can instruct and enlighten them. Some of the old Saiva saints, whose writings and stories now form part of the Saiva canon, fall into this category. Finally in the highest category are those very rare souls who realize the Self through the power of the Self within. Ramana Maharishi was of the third kind.

For most people today it is safe to assume that they belong neither to the second nor third category of seekers mentioned above. Hence for them, the grace of a human Satguru is mandatory for their spiritual journey. But as mentioned in the earlier sections, it takes several lifetimes to find a true Satguru. The best path is to sincerely carry on one's sadhana and wait patiently, rather than hurry into a wrong arrangement, which proves detrimental. Finally, as one reaches closer to the Self, the Self in its infinite kindness sends a Satguru to the sadhaka, who can channel the grace of the Divine—something a true Satguru is immensely capable of doing.

Inner Guru

For most people, navigating the spiritual path without a Guru is extremely difficult, if not impossible. For some, however, it may be possible, or at least a large part of the journey can be traversed if they are pure enough to be able to listen and follow the advice of their inner guide, who resides in the depth of the spiritual heart. The prompts we get from this inner Guru normally come to us in the form of 'viveka'—the discriminating power to sift out the untruthful from the truthful and that bypasses our reasoning. While it may be loud and clear in some, it can be faint and covered in a pool of other vices based on desires and conditioning. How then does one determine if an instruction is coming from this source or some other member of the being? The test is simple— observe the results. When one is guided by viveka, the Seeker is rewarded richly, one finds that the obstacles from their path are automatically removed, and a general sanguine happiness will pervade the soul. For one who can follow his viveka at all times without allowing sentiments or biases to cloud judgment, will soon find himself walking, to borrow a phrase from Sri Aurobindo, a 'sunlight path' through life. But that is the ideal situation, which rarely occurs. Most of us have not sufficiently detoxified ourselves of our own opportunistic nature, personal preferences and desires, to have the strength and courage needed to hear the voice of viveka clearly, and then follow it in without doubt or hesitation.

In some very rare cases, like that of Sri Aurobindo, one may get an adesha or command, but its nature is very different from the soft, clear prodding of viveka through the heart. An adesha is like an imperative which cannot be ignored, nor disobeyed, except maybe at the risk of physical discomfort if it is not followed through. This is not a normal occurrence among spiritual seekers. In the old Nath traditions, the yogis would specifically create or energize a subtle chakra by their sadhana, through which this command of their Guru or Lord would come to them. All these experiences cannot come to a Seeker at random, not until he has already silenced his mind completely—even then it may not happen to everyone. Again, as in the previous case, the true test of any adesha is the result one gets after following it.

A word of caution must be mentioned here. In certain paths which require special yogic exercises of controlled breathing like pranayama, or Tantra Sadhana, handholding from an authentic Guru is irreplaceable. These are highly technical paths with strict rules and regulations. They simply cannot be mastered without a good individualized mentor. Otherwise, the role of viveka is paramount in every aspect of spiritual life. It can also save an individual in difficult situations, even the darkest corners of the astral world, for it acts as both a guide and a protector.

Then there are those sadhakas who aim to realize the Self, which is perhaps the most difficult of all spiritual endeavours. If this is truly the deepest desire, and one must be honest about it, then one need not worry about a Guru at all. Just keep moving closer to the Self in every way that one can, by meditation or surrender, and as soon as one comes within a relative proximity (not in a spatial sense) to the Self, be sure the Self will send the appropriate Guru to push the Seeker into that zone. This is an unfailing spiritual dictum which has never been violated, for the Self is not an automation, it has a consciousness too, *chit shakti*, a divine *buddhi*, and it decides for itself when someone must be pulled inside its supernal atmosphere, or when not to do so. And if the Self decides to call a Seeker, no power in the universe can stop the sadhaka anymore. He is made.

Parameters of Judgment

Like in any other field, it is vital to judge our own spiritual progress in an objective manner. There are a few qualities which improve when the sadhana is working: an abiding peace, quietude, equanimity, calmness, unconditional love for the Divine, lack of desires or incessant striving, a steady courage in the face of all situations and circumstances born of a sanguine understanding that a higher force is in control of proceedings, and eventually, a steady power. But the greatest and safest sign of true spiritual growth is the reduction of the ego, for all the rest work only to the extent that the ego has been transplanted by something more universal in nature. The final elimination of ego is the greatest triumph possible, for this one simple sounding yet extremely difficult act opens the doors of Divine consciousness for the sadhaka. But before reaching this ultimate step one can also check to see if there is a corresponding decrease in the influence of the eight *pashas* or chains that bind consciousness—aversion, shame, pity, suspicion (or fear), hatred, and (pride of) family, (of) character, and (of) community.

In the very second chapter of the Bhagavad Gita, Arjuna enquires the signs of the man in *samadhi*, whose intelligence is firmly fixed in wisdom. How does the sage of settled understanding speak, how does he sit, how does he walk? And Sri Krishna replies:

दुखेष्वनुद्विग्रमनाः सुखेषु विगतः स्पृहः
वीतराग भय क्रोधः स्थितधीः मुनिरुच्यते

(He whose mind is undisturbed in the midst of sorrows and amid pleasures is free from desire,
From whom liking and fear and wrath have passed away, is the sage of settled understanding.)

यः सर्वत्रान अभिस्नेहस्तत्तत् प्राप्य शुभाशुभम्
न अभिनन्दति न द्वेष्टि तस्य प्रज्ञा प्रतिष्ठिता

(Who in all things is without affection though visited by this good or that

evil and neither hates nor rejoices, his intelligence sits firmly founded on
wisdom.)

यदा संहरते चायं कूर्मो अङ्गानीव सर्वशः
इन्द्रियाणीन्द्रियार्थेभ्यः तस्य प्रज्ञा प्रतिष्ठिता

(Who draws away the senses from the objects of sense, as the tortoise
draws in his limbs into the shell, his intelligence sits firmly founded in
wisdom.)

There are many other spiritual classics which have explained
the same core ideas that must be kept in mind if one is to make
genuine progress, and yet most of us today use 'experiences' as
a means for judging spirituality. That can be used to measure
spiritual growth, but only when taken in the proper context of the
previous parameters, and never in isolation. To be able to discern
a useful and genuine experience from a figment of imagination or
delusion, requires an exceptional inner clarity, which is rare in most
people, and almost never appears in seekers at the beginning of
their spiritual journey. Again, in such circumstances the closeness
to a genuine Guru can be very helpful, for like in most aspects of
life, firsthand experience and wisdom of a true preceptor can mean
the difference between actual spiritual growth and an imagined
spiritual fantasy. Keeping these simple and clear statements from
the Gita in mind one can help to set the direction right for any
Seeker and avoid any pitfalls, or at least be aware when things are
not going as planned.

The Intermediate Zone:
An Area of Darkness

There is a very wide zone, which Sri Aurobindo referred to as the 'intermediate zone', where the Seeker maybe suddenly introduced to exceptional experiences, of lights and sounds, and deities play into confirmation biases of varying degrees of exceptionalism, yet most of it is an illusion, a chimera designed to throw the *sadhaka* off the right path of growth.

This is what Sri Aurobindo wrote about this treacherous area:

All these experiences are of the same nature and what applies to one applies to another. Apart from some experiences of a personal character, the rest are either idea-truths, such as pour down into the consciousness from above when one gets into touch with certain planes of being, or strong formations from the larger mental and vital worlds which, when one is directly open to these worlds, rush in and want to use the sadhaka for their fulfilment. These things, when they pour down or come in, present themselves with a great force, a vivid sense of inspiration or illumination, much sensation of light and joy, an impression of widening and power. The sadhaka feels freed from the normal limits, projected into a wonderful new world of experience, filled and enlarged and exalted; what comes associates itself, besides, with his aspirations, ambitions, notions of spiritual fulfillment and Yogic siddhi; it is represented even as itself that realization and fulfillment. Very easily he is carried away by the splendor and the rush and thinks that he has realized more than he has truly done, something final or at least something sovereignly true. At this stage the necessary knowledge and experience are usually lacking which would tell him that this is only a very uncertain and mixed beginning; he may not realise at once that he is still in the cosmic Ignorance, not in the cosmic Truth, much less in the Transcendental Truth, and that whatever formative or dynamic idea-truths may have come down into him are partial only and yet further diminished by their presentation to him by a still mixed consciousness. He may fail to realise also that if he rushes to apply what he is realising or receiving as if it were something definitive, he may either fall into confusion and error or else get shut up in some partial formation in which there may be an element of spiritual Truth but it is likely to be outweighed by more dubious mental and vital accretions that deform it altogether. It is only when he is able to draw back (whether at once or after a time) from his experiences, stand above them with the dispassionate witness consciousness, observe their real nature, limitations, composition, mixture that he can proceed on his way towards a real freedom and a higher, larger and truer siddhi. At each step, this has to be done. For whatever comes in this way to the sadhaka of this yoga, whether it be from overmind or Intuition or Illumined Mind or some exalted Life Plane or from all these together, it is not definitive and final; it is not the supreme Truth in which he can rest, but only a stage. And yet these stages have to be passed through, for the supramental or the Supreme Truth cannot be reached in one bound or even in many bounds; one has to pursue a calm, patient and steady progress through many intervening stages without getting bound or attached to their lesser Truth or Light or Power or Ananda. This is, in fact, an intermediary state, a zone of transition between the ordinary consciousness in mind and the true yoga knowledge. One may cross without hurt through it, perceiving at once or at an early stage its real nature and refusing to be detained by its half-lights and tempting but imperfect and often mixed and misleading experiences; one may go astray in it, follow false voices and mendacious guidance, and that ends in a spiritual disaster; or one may take up one's abode in this intermediate zone, care to go no farther and build there some half-truth which one takes for the whole truth or become the instrument of the powers of these transitional planes—that is what happens to many sadhakas and Yogis.

It is very important to keep the above caveat in mind, for quite often when one starts serious *sadhana*, it propels the individual first into this grey area of half-truths, and any experience that comes from here is best not paid heed to as it deludes more than it can help. At any rate, the safest way out of this zone is to keep the parameters of judgment in mind, as mentioned in time-tested and universal spiritual classics like the Gita. Otherwise, any subjective experience howsoever grand and sublime it may be, is of no value until it also causes a corresponding change at the behavioural level of the individual Seeker. The development of inner light and protection that comes from a well-functioning *viveka* within a sadhaka can help pass this zone safely without damage or depreciation.

Another common misconception among sadhakas is that the duration of sadhana by itself indicates great advancement on the path. This is not at all the case. Far more important than duration is the direction of sadhana, and the ability to safely digest the Shakti generated by the sadhana. It is much easier to create Shakti than to integrate it with the mind and body, for that needs tremendous self-discipline in thoughts, words, and deeds. Consequently, sitting for long hours and performing vigorous rituals are no sanguine test of spiritual digestion or even growth. Remember that our shastras mention how asuras are known to have practised fantastic sadhana, which is unthinkable for humans or even gods, and yet they are neither respected nor looked upon as an ideal for spiritual growth.

In most cases and for a very long part of the journey, it is best to keep in mind the fundamental signs which must manifest if a true spiritual consciousness or change is appearing inside the Seeker. The legendary physicist Richard Feynman had once remarked, 'Science is a way of trying not to fool yourself.' This may apply easily to the spiritual path as well.

Asuric Sadhana

⚜

A *sadhana* that is practised for enhancement of one's own ego becomes asuric. But the same *sadhana* can become pure and in the true spirit of *adhyatma* when it is done as a sacrifice to reach the Divine. Of course, that is not easy and hence very few reach the highest zones, but then no great spiritual text has ever claimed the journey to be a cakewalk. Instead, the Upanishads firmly declare this journey as not only difficult but as dangerous as walking on a razor's edge.

The sixteenth chapter of the Gita delves into the differences between an asuric nature and a Divine nature.

आत्म संभाविताः स्तब्धा धन मान मदान्विताः
यजन्ते नामयज्ञैस्ते दंभेनविधिपूर्वकं

(They sacrifice and give not in the true order, but from a self-regarding ostentation, from vanity and with a stiff and foolish pride.)

त्रिविधं नरकस्येदं द्वारं नाशनमात्मनः
कामः क्रोधः तथा लोभः तस्मादेतत् त्रयं त्रयं त्यजेत्

(Threefold are the doors of Hell, destructive of the soul — desire, wrath, and greed: therefore, let man renounce these three.)

While going more deeply into an analysis of asuric sadhana is beyond the scope of this current book, suffice it to say that any sadhana done for the conscious or subconscious objective of ego-enhancement is asuric in nature and temperament. Many people believe that certain kinds of Shakta sadhakas, particularly those who are of the tantric disposition are engaging in asuric sadhana. This is quite untrue, for in that case, no great saint would have come from the tantric *paramparas*. Even someone as revered as Sri Ramakrishna had performed all the 64 sadhanas of Tantra and realized the truth in that path. It is not the sadhana per se by which we may judge whether something is of a Divine nature or of an asuric nature, but the effect that the sadhana has on the Seeker, and then through the Seeker onto his connected surroundings. Something as innocuous as meditation can become a deadly and negative force if it causes an unchecked, delusional and dangerous increase in the ego. This is precisely why every ritual in all paths ends with a process of dedication of the ritual and its fruits to the deity or the Guru.

Anugraha

The most elusive of all spiritual forces is *anugraha* or Grace. It cannot be humanly controlled, neither begged, nor forced or extracted by any known means. Even the Guru cannot control Grace. It originates in the Divine and at the opportune moment it flows to the Seeker, sometimes through the agency of the Guru but not in a willed manner, or by any other means which involves a spiritual straining in the Seeker. Without Grace, the journey is never completed, but there is no specific ritual that can bring Grace into the life of the Seeker. Ramakrishna used to say that Grace is like the wind that is eternally blowing, one must raise his sails to catch its effects. It belongs to no one, but is for everyone, for it is Divine in nature.

There is a lower *prakriti* in man and nature, which works through the automated movements of cosmic forces on the prana shakti of an individual, without the individual consciously realizing from where they originate. This is different from the higher prakriti which resides in the more self-conscious and Divine. The manifestation in a human being of this lower prakriti happens in the form of rage, lust, compulsive possessiveness, greed, vital passions, etc. For the purpose of transforming oneself, these lower, forceful instinctive movements of one's lower nature need to be controlled and eventually rejected. The vital body (*pranamaya-kosha*) is a pure force, constant in movement, dynamic in nature, but lacking in light and wisdom, (light here being synonymous with knowledge). At the higher spiritual levels, perfect knowledge (*gyanshakti*) and will (*ichchashakti*) are fused together and work in harmony. But in our plane of existence, these two have become separated and distorted. Therefore, often you may have the will to achieve something but not the right knowledge needed for it, which leads to a sense of frustrating incapacity.

Grace is the result of a total and complete surrender made from the mind, life and body. These three also correspond to those parts of the human consciousness working in and through the *manomaya-kosha* (the mental sheath), pranamaya-kosha (the vital sheath) and *annamaya-kosha* (the physical sheath). Until this sense of unqualified total surrender is reached, Grace does not come, and even if it does, it gets perverted and distorted by the inferior nature. In the Gita Sri Krishna calls it *apara-prakriti*, that part of nature which functions by the diktats of the three *gunas—satva*, *raja*, and *tamas*. It is one thing to say verbally that all sadhana being done is the work of God. It is an entirely different matter to see it clearly, for which one must first surrender constantly, then reject and withdraw one's inferior nature, or at least keep it calm and restrained, and finally make a sincere call to the Divine. Only when these three work together, Grace descends. And only Grace has the power to cause a thorough transformation of a sadhaka. Nothing less can make this possible. But we can't demand Grace, we can't beg for it, we can't plead, we can't command, and we can't indulge in self-pity. We must calmly and patiently wait for it because only when the time is right, it falls like sweet rain on a parched land, and in a flash, it can do more than what we can imagine in our wildest dreams.

Our first job, therefore, is to move away from our own peculiar Pavlovian instincts and allow that Grace of higher power to work unhindered. It is this power, once understood, that one needs to submit to unquestioningly in a progressive manner while rejecting everything else inside the Seeker that pulls one in a different direction and causes them to hang on to the earlier, flawed personality. This is certainly a long road, but patience is key.

Experience vs Realization

⟡

Quite often when an individual starts *sadhana*, there is an initial flood of interesting experiences. Some of them can be genuine, and some the figment of an overactive imagination. But mostly it is a characteristic of spiritual journey. However, it is a capital mistake to take those experiences as final and definitive because one is not yet at the condition where one may judge accurately which is a real and helpful experience and which may be a misleading experience created by the ego-mind. This is where a Guru or a mentor is extremely helpful. A Guru can ground the *sadhaka* and tell him what to focus on and what to reject. A helpful thumb-rule is not to get too attached or overawed by experiences, particularly those which appear too grandiose. Also, any experience that breaks the asana of the sadhaka is something to be wary of.

Oftentimes, the experiences that occur in one's spiritual journey maybe due to the innate lack of containment within the

Seeker instead of the absence of expertise in the matter. During the time of Sri Ramakrishna, people around him would often come to him and describe various interesting spiritual experiences they would have, and Ramakrishna would encourage and guide them appropriately. Seeing all this, one day Naren, who had not yet taken sanyasa, came to him and complained as to why he did not get as many experiences as the others despite being near the master. In his typical style, Ramakrishna used an analogy to explain. He said that most people were like small tanks where the movement of a big fish caused water to spill over, while he was like a huge pond where fishes could run around as much as they liked yet it wouldn't cause the slightest ripple on the surface of the water. Effectively, he was talking about the concept of *adhara* in spirituality—the mind-body complex of the Seeker. The number of experiences and extent of spiritual force that an individual can contain is always constrained by the limits of the adhara. One possessing a weak adhara won't be able to digest an experience easily and that may cause him to go overboard and react excessively, while one who has a larger and stronger adhara will digest experiences without any sound or noise breaking to the surface.

The ideal state is not to deny the experience, neither to crave for it nor get overexcited by it but watch it as silently as possible. Observe and record everything but be attached to nothing. Whenever a disciple would come to Ramana Maharishi speaking about any spiritual experience, be it visions or sounds, Maharishi would ask, Is it still there? If not, this cannot be God, for God is a constant who does not fluctuate. When he comes, he remains permanently.

There's many a slip 'twixt the cup and the lip. Beyond experiences stand realization. That means integrating the result of the experience permanently inside the personality. Oftentimes this requires a change in the consciousness of a Seeker, for an experience or Shakti of a higher plane will not share space with the consciousness of a lower mold. Practically, this is the most difficult aspect for sadhakas in this age and time. People crave for an experience but those are relatively easy to get if the rules of sadhana are followed diligently. But what happens after an experience? An honest appraisal of the results would show a tendency of the previous behaviour patterns, thoughts, habits, etc., all coming back in time, maybe not immediately but certainly in months and years. This is an effect of the Shakti that probably entered the individual during the experience, assuming it was a genuine experience, leaving the adhara because the individual could not digest it properly, causing permanent change in the fundamental aspects.

The basic parameters of spiritual growth—peace, calm, detachment, equanimity, steady courage, or a feeling of Divine love—remain constant, whatever be the source or nature of the experience and the Shakti that caused it. If some or all of these parameters increase, know that the experience has caused a change inside; if not, such experiences are futile and unhelpful in progress. Sometimes a specific ability may come to a Seeker due to an experience. That too is a tangible result, but it must be verified objectively. However, making a permanent change inside so that the new energy is settled within requires great.discipline and care, especially during the initial phase of nurturing. It may require control of food and sleep, staying away from any individual or situation that disrupts the conscious feeling of the change. A certain degree of aloofness from the world is very important. Every Seeker passes through this phase. But when such a conducive environment is not produced, this new energy will wear off due to frictions from a hostile environment, and soon enough old habits and patterns will resurface again, and the progress will turn into regress. In these cases, again, a good mentor or Guru can be very helpful in guiding the sadhaka.

Varieties of Experience

The nature of experiences that a sadhaka may witness initially has a lot to do with one's psychological makeup as well as their *purva samskaras* and the path they are walking. For some, it may come in the manner of visions, or sounds, or forms or light. Every form of a deity is an inspired archetype, which contains the symbolic details of the devata's functionality, nature and the path to reach that form. Other times there could be specific sounds and the specific smell of substances which are associated with a particular deity. Sometimes these may be subjective in the sense that only the Seeker can experience it. At other times the manifestation may be so strong that anyone in the surrounding environment will also witness some experience, even though they may not be able to comprehend it properly. Sometimes a Seeker may not see the form of a deity but only see the light of the deity. Whatever way a deity appears to the Seeker, the important thing is that it can leave a strong impact within for sure. In some cases, there are recorded evidence of deities appearing in a physical form too, either human or animal. Particularly in some Shakta rituals the appearance of the Divine Shakti happens through the agency of an animal. Depending on the specific animal that appears, it is taken as indicative of the actualization of the ritual's aim. However, having a direct and final experience of a deity, particularly one of the great ones like Shiva or Vishnu or Devi is not easy. It may need some serious inner transformation beforehand.

Quite often, it is a projection of a deity created in the astral plane by the sadhana of the Seeker which may appear first. This is the fundamental basis of much of Tantra and *mantra sadhana*. The mantra is the body of the deity and along with accurate visualizations, which the Guru can teach the disciple, and by repeated concentration, *homas, tarpana,* etc., eventually a formation of the deity is created by the mental and pranic Shakti of the sadhaka. This formation will have a life of its own and interact with the sadhaka exactly in the same way that another independent individual interacts. If the process is accurately followed then this astral formation will even display supernatural ability, appropriate to the deity, and help and guide the Seeker on the path. Eventually, one day, if it is so destined, this formation can take the Seeker into the realm of the actual deity and merge inside. This is the perfection or *siddhi* of deity sadhana.

Sometimes a deity may reside inside the physical body of the sadhaka, provided it is pure enough to hold the Shakti, or the Seeker's mind will enter into a communion with the mind stream of the deity. In that condition whatever a Seeker does is an act of the deity where the sadhaka is but an instrument or a vehicle of that superior power.

Given the complexity of the mechanics described above, not all experiences of a deity are helpful to spiritual growth. Sometimes an experience may even come without any immediate cause, but likely due to desires and efforts from past lives. The important question, and probably this is the only fundamental question a Seeker must keep asking oneself: did the experience cause a sustained spiritual change? If not (which is what happens in a vast majority of cases when a casual or one-off experience with a deity happens) then one must keep doing more sadhana. To give an example, when Ramakrishna had a vision of Kali in Dakshineswar it changed him permanently. But there are many others worshiping the same deity, having occasional glimpses or even experiences. While those may be beautiful in their own way but practically end up causing no sustainable change from their previous thought and behaviour patterns. Not all 'seeing' is the same, no two interactions with the world of deities are equal. In some cases, the interaction with a deity can be dangerous in much the same way that without sufficient knowledge and protection if one were to enter the ambit of a wild animal. Interacting with them without sound understanding of this may lead to unintended, and at times, even detrimental consequences for the Seeker.

In any case, it is vital to remember that a truly transformative experience of a deity, like what Ramakrishna had, does not come about until the Seeker has worked on removing his own weakness and flaws of habit and nature. This of course is no simple matter. It is the most boring part of the spiritual journey, but also perhaps the most difficult. Sri Aurobindo would state categorically that rejection is an integral part of sadhana. The ability to reject from oneself and one's environment, all that is wrong, ignorant, base and detrimental to a true change in consciousness is a prerequisite before a new energy or Shakti takes residence inside the adhara.

In some cases (and these are indeed rare) a Seeker may experience no deity but enter into an indefinable, formless and timeless condition, or have an experience of the atma. Though this may feel different, yet this too must be passed through the same kind of rigorous judgment before accepting it as authentic and genuine. Have the previous behaviour patterns and flaws reduced and vanished? Is there an increase in the characteristics that reflect a true spiritual growth? How can the change be made permanent?

All powerful spiritual experiences finally boil down to two areas of the body. Behind the heart and above the head. The Upanishads mentioned the presence of a thumb-sized being deep inside the heart which governs our life, around which the physical, vital and mental body, or sheath develops and helps us interact with the world around. This entity truly recognizes the Divine, and never falls into missteps or gets awed by appearances without substance. And above the head is a vast area of limitless silence and freedom—freedom of the *chit shakti* from the caged existence of a physical human body. These two are the best gateways to a genuine, real and helpful engagement with the eternal path, Sanatana Dharma.

Inner Silence

The greatest step to the realm of the Divine is quietude and inner silence. Whatever be the path, whatever be the deity or the sadhana, the normal mind, which keeps working by a labour of friction of ideas, can never really enter into the truly *adhyatmik* realms. It always adds and divides into pieces, thinks only a limited number of possibilities; it can assimilate to a point but not beyond—even its imagination is borrowed from a substratum of limited subjective experience. The Divine is completely beyond the scope of the normal mind even in its wildest imagination. The *Kenopanishad* explains by asking the most important of all spiritual questions:

who directs the mind, who commands prana, who is the source of speech? To define Brahma is to deny Brahma; Satchidananda is but a provisional definition. How can the mind ever know this? Even the sharpest minds fail to capture the Divine in its full potential and manifesting power. What then is the solution? Yogis first calm the mind completely, making it still and then the still mind slowly allows a glimpse into what lies beyond. In a disturbed lake the bottom remains invisible; only when the water becomes still can someone see what lies beneath or beyond. It is the same for the human mind. When inner silence, or at least a quietness, becomes deeper and more integrated, the Divine becomes perceptible to the Seeker in some manner. Before that, the mind is merely imagining the Divine from secondhand knowledge, book reading or hearing from others. The gateway to real spirituality passes through the doors of nirvana, which is effectively an absolute cessation of mental fluctuations.

One may wonder: how does one act and work in life when the mind is stopped? Sri Aurobindo poignantly observed that whatever can be done by the mind, can be done better in the silence of the mind. In that condition, a natural governance is established of the Self or Divine, which then uses the undisturbed mind merely as a conduit to pass information or instruction as needed by the individual to act effectively in any situation.

However, a one-off experience of the nirvanic condition is not enough. It must be permanent, else the mind germinates again, with all its flaws and unhealthy patterns of behaviour. On the other hand, if someone were to abide by an inner silence under all conditions, they would radiate a special spiritual Shakti which can calm down others, or even automatically resolve problems. Silence is the language which Shiva as Dakshinamurti used to transmit the highest teachings to the four sages who came to him for advice.

Often people seem to believe that verbal silence can help produce great effects. Verbal silence is certainly a very useful sadhana, but it is only secondary to mental silence. However, in the event that the latter is still far, it is a useful practice to try and follow verbal silence for some period at least. But this indeed is the true hallmark of a mature sadhaka.

Purusha and Prakriti

In all our spiritual literature, one of the most fundamental ideas is the duality of Purusha and Prakriti. In general, in the older spiritual traditions from the Upanishadic era to the Bhagavad Gita, the Purusha—especially the immutable Purusha—was considered the goal of the journey. We use the word Purusha to mean a male in general, but spiritually Purusha's primary quality is stillness and control. From that stillness comes true knowledge and understanding, and the ability to organize the knowledge systematically.

Prakriti in its most generic understanding is nature that governs the physical world. In its spiritual understanding, Prakriti is but a form of Shakti, only more mechanical in its process, whereas Shakti is conscious. The same energy as it moves towards unconsciousness becomes Prakriti, and when it moves towards consciousness becomes Shakti. Without Shakti no manifestation is possible. In the highest realms, Shakti is the dynamic power of the Brahma while Purusha is the static condition of the Brahma. Or Shakti is the projection of the Purusha's power, but in the world we inhabit, which is anyway far distanced from the highest spiritual realms, the operation of Purusha and Shakti appear to be significantly different. In the later schools of spirituality, particularly the Tantras, we find Shakti being accorded more prominence than Purusha.

But both are equally important for complete spiritual development and must function in tandem. The importance of Shakti lies in the fact that without Shakti one cannot do anything useful in this world. Hence, the dictum used in Tantras: Shiva without Shakti is like *shava* or a dead body.

However, while the usefulness of Shakti is a certain fact, but this knowledge, if not sufficiently qualified, is useless for spiritual growth. Not all kinds of Shakti is good for a Seeker; he must have the ability to discern so as to know which one can take him into spirituality, and avoid the rest. It also becomes vital in most paths to find an anchor for this power, a handle using which this Shakti can be safely used to navigate the path. This is where the Purusha *tattva* becomes critical. In the ideal spiritual condition, the Purusha gives the command, and Shakti executes that command. Like a boat in an ocean, Shakti is the power of the engine, without which one has no chance of moving anywhere, but Purusha is the rudder of the boat that provides direction to the Seeker, else one can keep moving for countless lifetimes and yet reach nowhere. In later spiritual literature, Purusha tattva became equated with Lord Shiva while Shakti manifested as various forms of devis, each with specialized attributes and ability.

Spirituality of the Intellect

⥤⟶⥻⟵⥢

One of the oft-repeated assertions in spiritual circles is that the mind and intellect are a hindrance to true spirituality. This is only partially true, an oversimplification of the problem due to a misunderstanding of the intellect's true nature and function.

The mind is but a loose term for a collection of various psychological processes of a human being. It can be broadly classified into three parts. First the sensory mind, also called *manas*, which controls and reacts to the influences that reach the mind through the sense organs. This part of the mind is driven by instinctive reactions. Then the *chitta*, which is like a repository of all impressions and influences. Everything that a human being ever does, howsoever insignificant, plants an impression in the chitta. At odd times, in otherwise uncalled for situations, the chitta can throw up random, arbitrary images from a half-forgotten past, which can break the concentration of a *sadhaka*. A significant part of the spiritual purification is purifying the chitta. The third part of the mind is a mental *ahamkara*. It is a very subtle I-sense which opposes endlessly and mindlessly, sometimes in a secret and subliminal manner, whenever there is an attempt to transform the mind by the process of *sadhana*. The ahamkara will do just about anything to hang on to the old personality including its various likes, dislikes, automatic movements, passions, desires, comfort zones, etc., for only by the survival of the normal personality can the ahamkara's own existence be justified. Often people wrongly translate the word ahamkara to mean pride. Pride is just one manifestation of it; expressions of humility, pity or even friendship (or any human relation) can also be a work of the ahamkara. Any refusal to change the ignorant nature of the surface personality is a work of the ahamkara fighting for self-preservation.

From the chitta is projected another aspect of the mind, which is the realm of pure thoughts. This is buddhi. In most people the *buddhi* part of the mind is inseparably tied to the *manas*, the chitta and ahamkara. Therefore, the thought process is driven in a very subjective manner by the randomness of the conditioning present in the chitta or the compulsive, reactive nature of the manas, or is taken for a royal ride by the ahamkara churning out comfortable but insincere logic to justify its own peculiar biases. The buddhi thus becomes severely distorted and defeats the very purpose of its own existence. Such a mind becomes a terrible master.

On the other hand, if buddhi is taught to function without being influenced by the sensory mind or the repository of random impressions and conditioned thinking, to be free from the influence of the ahamkara, then it can work in an objective and non-distorted fashion, searching for the truth as it is. Such an intellect, unspoiled and pure, is never outraged by anything for agitation is foreign to its nature; it can look at all possibilities however obnoxious or repugnant in complete calmness and weigh each side using well-defined parameters of judgement. In a Vedantic interpretation one may say that the Rig Vedic rishis named this pure intellect as Indra, one who has won the battle against *indriyas* (sensory mind, manas), the mighty slayer of the demon *vritra* (meaning envelop), and hence named *vritahan*.

Once this pure intellect is developed and instilled and one learns to operate from that platform of perfection, one must ideally head for the next stage of pushing the frontiers of the mind and intellect into a higher region of functioning, where the intellect can integrate apparently contradictory lines of thought in a harmonious manner by default. Even higher than this stage is an intellect with a natural illumination and unfailing intuition, which can know things by dint of a process that seems to bypass normal logical constructs. Beyond this intuitive mind lies the realm of the great gods, where like a universal game of chess one sees innumerable possibilities on every side, near-infinite karmic chains and their exact repercussions right down to the minutest details. It functions not from the premise of piecemeal building blocks of reason, for such a lower method simply cannot handle a complexity of such proportions but from a perspective of spontaneous knowledge that does not need to strive. Still further is a mind where direct knowledge of Truth comes by the inalienable oneness of subject and object, of the viewer and the viewed, or the experiencing agent and the experienced subject, where everything is simultaneously and equally divided yet undivided. There is no point thinking of it from our normal mind because it is way beyond the farthest reaches of imagination.

The one disadvantage of the intellect is its habit of moving in endless circles when it hits a logical roadblock. If one falls into that trap, the intellect hinders the Seeker's progress. However, if one is well aware of the limits of pure intellect, one can very well use it as a stepping stone into a higher range of the mind and beyond. But to imbibe the essence of these higher platforms of the intellect, one must first develop pure intellect—uncluttered by manas, chitta and *aham*, which is the beginning of the spiritual plane. And therein lies the problem, for humans are rational and objective only in name, while in reality, we are still often irrational. Without breaking away from the clutches of manas and chitta, the pure intellect cannot soar to the higher regions and will remain more a hindrance than help in the spiritual development of a Seeker. Whereas an intellect which has overcome the influence of the senses, indriyas, become a lord of the whole being in the same way as Indra is the lord of the devas.

Sampradaya:
Uses and Limitations

We are often told that everything in spirituality is based on the *sampradaya*. This is true but only with some caveats. Our primary texts, especially the Upanishads and the Gita, do not mention any sampradaya by name but deal directly with statements concerning spiritual matters. The Vedantic sampradayas were born from interpreting these texts in the light of different philosophies based on the experience of the originator of each sampradaya. So, to a Shankara his *bhasyas* and interpretation of the texts are the Vedanta, whereas the bhakti sampradayas consider their own interpretation as the ultimate truth in this matter.

Shankaracharya used terms like *asampradayavid* in his Gita bhasyas for anyone who does not adhere to his understanding, and even went to the extent of chastising all those who engage in the *upasana* of forms, which he thought, as per some parts of the commentary on Gita, as a lower kind of upasana. Naturally, the scholars of the later day bhakti schools have given it back to Shankara and his system with equal force and harshness, rejecting it outright as a form of disguised Buddhism. Some even went to the extent of calling Shankara the incarnation of a *rakshasa*. While Adwaitins believe their system accommodates all, it is only a partial truth because it accommodates philosophies like Dvaita by providing a lower status to the system. It never says both or all paths are equally true; it is a bit like saying, I tolerate you, but I am clear that you are inferior. The other Vedantic schools are exclusivist; they reject Advaita entirely.

It is important to remember that every sampradaya is finally born at a point in history mostly by the spiritual and metaphysical genius of some institution-builder. But all of them, even the hoariest, are far removed from the time when the men who composed the primary texts lived. That is Vyasa or Badrayana or Krishna. So, all the various flavours of Vedantic sampradayas are relatively new endeavours in a given long enough timescale.

The power of a sampradaya comes by repetition of sadhana and by their ability to produce spiritual men and women using the philosophy and doctrines followed therein. That is how the authenticity and veracity of a sampradaya is established in time. While the philosophy provides the superstructure of a sampradaya, it is the living tradition of practical sadhana and the saints produced by the lineage, which holds the sampradaya and its followers together. Right after Adi Shankaracharya, the first real critique of Shankara's interpretation came from a scholar named Bhaskara. But Bhaskara never created a system of sadhana, therefore his analysis and interpretation of the Brahma Sutras are largely forgotten except among scholars of Hinduism.

Each sampradaya is susceptible to a single weak link in the chain of transmission. Nobody can fix this; that is how matters transpire. The classic example given is that of one great pundit who had a cat and would tie that cat near his puja room when he sat for puja so that the animal did not disturb him. Few generations down the line nobody really remembered why he used to tie the cat, the thought process, and that action transformed into a dogma and a new rule was made that whoever did that puja ought to first buy one cat for himself and then tie it near the room!

There are many good things in sampradaya too. Best of which is the tested practice, a process that has been applied before on others and which has produced verifiable results and then the practice is passed down in the line of transmission. In Shakta systems it is even more invaluable because each new generation is like a leaf in a tree whose roots are the Kuladevatas, guiding the process. Like in one sampradaya based out of a famous spiritual town of North India, it is a tradition to bring back (they know how to do so) their old masters, so that wherever they may be born they will come back to that place and continue their sadhana. That said given a long enough timescale, old sampradayas start to disintegrate and new sampradayas are born from that dispersion. That too is an unalterable law of nature. Eventually one day the new sampradayas grow old, spread their roots, and become the next unquestionable orthodoxy.

Every time a new sampradaya is born there will be resistance from the old. This is basic human nature. Most of the resistance is not based on sound logic, but a vital and egoistic obstinacy, born from insecurity. Sri Ramanujacharya's Advaita Guru tried to kill him. Shankara's interpretation was considered near heretical by Bhaskara, a contemporary philosopher of Shankara's era. Or, when

Madhva, whose name Tirtha points to his inclusion in the system started by Shankara, finally left that system, he became both a rule breaker (deviating from the older tradition) and the originator of a new tradition. But despite endless naysayers or jittery reaction of the orthodoxy, the survival and creation of new traditions within the fold of Sanatana Dharma are based on the spiritual truth and Shakti invested in the individual originator by larger forces of destiny.

Finally, there are genuine people within different sampradayas, just as there are genuine people who belong to no sampradaya. The true spiritual worth of an individual is not tied to his designations or the lack thereof. People who have reached a transformed condition, which can be verified, whether they belong to some sampradaya or not, recognize this fact organically. It is only the *mahamurkhas* (we have no dearth!) whether they be of a *sampradayic* persuasion or *asampradayic*, who believe that the Divine is confined to this or that tradition or to some form of orthodoxy or some nouveau heterodoxy. Each of these has a purpose and a scope; taken beyond that it becomes an error and finally a crippling idiocy. It is perfectly possible to attain spiritual help and transform without being part of any known sampradaya, just as it is amply evident that many great spiritual giants who have graced this land belonged to well-known sampradayas.

Rituals vs Jnana

There is an old conflict in Indian spirituality, more classically known as the dichotomy between Karmakanda and Jnanakanda, wherein the adherents of the two different schools born from the Vedic path argue about the importance and necessity of rituals vis-à-vis contemplative study and practice. Briefly, the first path is born from the belief held by the Mimamsaka philosophers that exact performance of the Vedic rituals is the chief Dharma or duty of an individual, and the power of the ritual by itself ensures a flowering of Dharma all around and a greater and favourable journey after death. The opposing camp devalued these rituals and believed that by mere performance of rituals one could achieve nothing significant, certainly not spiritual growth, which came only with a transcendence of habitual religious practice, ritualistic or otherwise. In this vein, we find in the Gita, Sri Krishna advising Arjuna that the Vedas are in the modes of the three *gunas*, whereas he, Arjuna, must transcend even these. Well, if the Vedas are unquestionably supreme, how can someone transcend these? Or did the thought-flow of the Gita not believe that the ritualism of the Vedas by default as sufficient to lead one to true spirituality? Some of the later Upanishads too categorically downplay the need for rituals or their efficacy in a spiritual life. This conflict is the base that explains best why the Buddha, and later Tantras, were also seen as anti-Vedic. By this, it will be wrong to construe that these two schools were opposed to everything about the Vedas. They opposed the ritualistic portions, while they imbibed the philosophical essence of the Upanishadic thought into their doctrines, often clothed in new terminology.

In modern times many associate the path of non-duality, particularly the new models of Advaita Vedanta, to have a strong predisposition against rituals. However, arising from the fact that until the mind and body have been extremely purified, non-ritualism very easily changes into a *tamasic* sloth and lethargy. And this is far more dangerous than whatever negatives, or incompleteness may enter a Seeker attached to a mechanical performance of rituals.

What then is a ritual? Any set of coordinated actions which bring a sense of meaning, purpose, energy, and direction to the spiritual life can be called a ritual. Of these, there are some which have been practised by ancients since ages and are known to produce transformative effects in the Seeker. Their efficacy is unquestionable. While the Tantra shastras rejected Vedic rituals, at times calling them snakes without poison, they however reinvented and revitalized rituals in their own path and laid extreme stress on rituals incorporated in the form of *sadhana*, or spiritual exertion, in order to take one closer to enlightenment. Repeated performance of a ritual when done with understanding and comprehension and faith in the deity and Guru (and sometimes both can be one), produces a change in the inner nature of the *sadhaka*. And this is a concrete spiritual progress.

The astral world that surrounds us leaves its imprint constantly on the physical. Sri Aurobindo used to say every great action or movement first happens in the ethereal planes and then comes down to our world. Similarly, every single energetic atmosphere on earth, whatever be the kind of energy, has a corresponding purer version of itself in the ethereal worlds. This principle is used by those who are experts in rituals. Every action, every ingredient used in a well-constructed ritual is symbolic of some Shakti, not merely as an intellectual substitute but also in a real sense. The final ritual is like cooking, add the right ingredients at the right time and in the right manner and a delightful dish is produced.

However, ritualism creates a problem when one engages in it without contemplation or understanding, as a mechanical activity to be performed for whatever reason and raises it to the rank of an unquestionable dogma. That leads to nothing more than further muddy delusions and bondage of the mind and is anathema to real *adhyatma*. In fact, the best practice involves employing a mixture of both karma and *jnana*, unless one is as special as a Ramana Maharishi, but then even Ramana from his dizzying heights of non-duality would still recommend people to do *pradakshina* of Shiva, who resides in the form of the holy ancient Arunachala! That too is a ritual, an enlightened one.

Self-Realization

❧❦❧

Everyone who has not realized the Self is nearly the same. But every self-realized individual is unique. Unlike the simplistic view propagated today, no two individuals who have realized the Self, experienced it in the exact same manner and depth, and it can't be properly expressed in words because it is difficult to verbalize the shades and degrees of experience—the gap between the speaker and the audience of the thought is almost unbridgeable— and therefore we are now constricted in our expression with the oversimplified word 'enlightenment'.

The error in understanding happens because we imagine self-realization to be something like sitting in a chair, or maybe entering a room—whoever gets in will have attained it, we think. But in reality, this is like jumping into a bottomless pool of water; some may swim on the surface, some go a bit deep, others may venture deeper, and some will plunge so deep that they won't come back to the surface again. But the moment you enter the pool, and if you so desire to communicate your experience to those who have not entered, you are struck by an amazing lack of vocabulary in any language to accurately convey what is going on. Therefore, many of the best masters choose silence. Whereof one cannot speak, thereof one must be silent.

Sat-Chit-Ananda

There are three fundamental attributes of the Brahman as per our oldest scriptures: *sat-chit-ananda*. Sat or *satya* means reality. Without going into complicated philosophical definitions of what is real and what is not, a simple definition, and which suffices well for our purposes, would be that whatever is unchanging is the greatest reality. This automatically excludes most of the world around, which is, of course, real in an immediate sense, but not so when viewed from the podium of non-dual realization.

Chit, the middle term, is the movement and force of consciousness, and *ananda* is restful bliss. Quite often, depending on the predisposition and *purva samskara* of the *sadhaka*, one enters into the Brahman through one of these three. The experience of an unchanging reality is generally the entry point experience into the Brahmic condition for a Seeker who does *tapas* by means of *jnana*. When yogic methods of *sadhana* are applied, whether it be breath-control, or specific mantras, or *kriyas*, etc., then the chit aspect of Brahman is experienced first. Finally, when pure unconditioned surrender or bhakti is used as a means to reach the Self, then the ananda aspect of the Divine comes to the Seeker first.

Bhakti, though it sounds simple and naive, is probably as difficult and rare as *jnana*. Any thought, desire or subtle expectation of immediate results tarnishes bhakti and makes it ineffective. The Divine is perfectly capable of seeing through the deepest recesses and the darkest corners of the human mind and heart. A devotion that manifests in words alone (verbal devotion) or done with pretence at heart fails to impress or bring results. It is easy to fool ourselves, not the Divine.

In the progression of the chapters covering different aspects of spirituality, the Gita brings bhakti after the Viswarupa is manifested before Arjuna. That grand, infinite vision reduced the hero of the Kuru clan into a state of fear and submission, for not only had he not seen anything like this before, it was perfectly beyond his ability to grasp and digest. When faced with something truly Divine the human mind reaches the limits of its processing ability, and the only meaningful way it can interact with such a tremendous reality is by means of surrender and devotion. Bhakti is there in every path. For *jnani* too is a bhakt of the Self. Complete and unconditional surrender is just as difficult as removing the I-sense by the power of *jnana tapas*. For most people, it is a combination of these paths that help to steer the boat of sadhana to safer shores.

On Karma Yoga

✦

Since the time Sri Krishna spoke the Gita on the battlefield of Kurukshetra, it has become one of the most important spiritual texts of Hinduism. Its language is simple, and its philosophy is wide and vast, covering different paths and yet uplifting them and still bringing something new into our spiritual worldview. Wise men and scholars have delineated the yoga of Gita into some basic paths: jnana yoga, bhakti yoga, karma yoga, where each one is often looked at as an independent path to one's yogic development.

During the British rule, when many great Indian revolutionaries were attracted to the idea of service to the motherland, karma yoga became perhaps the most widely used spiritual phrase to inspire a temperamentally slothful nation into severe and concentrated activity. Members of the Anushilan Samiti (Onushilon Somiti) would take an oath on the Gita before dedicating their lives to liberating India from British rule. Service to the nation, service to mankind and service for all were taken as the ultimate goal and practical manifestation of Krishna's advice to Arjuna. Not only the youth but also the leaders and thinkers of the previous century, mostly in a valiant attempt to enthuse a *tamas*-infected nation, took recourse to highlight the worker's role in both social and spiritual life.

Even today, in colloquial terms we use karma yoga, or the adjective karma yogi, to refer to any individual who is essentially a workaholic or someone with great time management skills who can get a lot of things accomplished, far more, than ordinary, or those who do a lot of selfless service for humanity. Appreciable no doubt, and very important as these things may be in enriching a human character, but we need to ask, is that all there is to karma yoga, or rather, is there any difference between a terrific tireless worker, and someone who works in the mode of yoga? These are appreciable qualities no doubt, but is karma yoga only about tirelessly working, or rather working with the detachment of a yogi?

Probably the most important, arguably, the only important text that speaks of this path to liberation—for it is indeed a path of yoga—is the Gita itself. The Gita, of course, is a *moksha shastra*, which means it gives greater primacy to spiritual enlightenment (a generic term for a range of rare powerful states) over other cardinal aims of life. In the very first chapter of the text, Arjuna Vishada yoga, we find a reluctant, pity-filled Arjuna refusing to fight against his relatives and gurus while proffering various excuses and arguments as to why this war is sinful and against Dharma, only to be rebuffed by Sri Krishna, who then explains to him the secret of yogic work, as also various other aspects of spiritual evolution.

A flawed understanding of karma has led Indians to believe that this is a mechanical law of give and take, of action and reaction, of crime and punishment, and there is no escaping it. By this logic Arjuna's frank refusal is certainly valid, for killing another, and that too his powerful gurus, is surely an act that can bring about great karmic repercussions. There was at least one famous spiritual Guru from western India who believed that this was indeed what Arjuna should have done—dropped his weapons and run to the forest to meditate. Well, there may be several misconceptions about the Gita and reading all sorts of angles from the text to suit and justify one's pre-conceived notions is not new, for even the great acharyas tried to find their ideas by selectively giving prominence to some verses in the text over others, or creatively interpreting the verses. And yet this particularly superficial suggestion that Arjuna should have dropped his weapons and left for a sanyasi's life is probably the most absurd misrepresentation of this ancient philosophy of life and works.

But even before Sri Krishna goes on to clear Arjuna's spiritual misgivings, he retorts to the warrior-hero's submission: 'I will not fight!', by explaining how the latter's words and actions do not align:

श्री भगवानुवाच
अशोच्यानन्वशोचस्त्वं प्रज्ञा वादां च भाषसे
गतासूनः अगतासूनः च नानुशोचन्ति पण्डिताः

(*The Blessed Lord said: Thou grievest for those that should not be grieved for, yet speakest words of wisdom. The enlightened man does not mourn either for the living or for the dead.*)

In another verse in the same chapter, Sri Krishna says that he will disclose the secret of yoga, after having explained Samkhya spirituality, wherein one can cast away the bondage created by karma.

एषा तेभिहिता साङ्ख्ये बुद्धिः योगेति इमां शृणु
बुद्ध्या युक्तो यया पार्थ कर्मबन्धं प्रहास्यसि

Of importance is the fact that in the actual text of the Gita, the word 'Samkhya' in effect is almost synonymous with the path that gives spiritual uplift through knowledge, jnana yoga, while the term yoga refers to the path of action, karma yoga, leading to the same goal. This may also be a reflection of how these terms were considered during the *sandhi* of Dwapara and Kali when the great 18-day war happened, which is certainly not the way we interpret these two terms today.

A few verses later we have the clearest and most profound statement of practical advice regarding karma yoga:

कर्मण्येवाधिकारस्ते मा फलेषु कदाचन
मा कर्म फल हेतुः भूः माते सङ्गोस्त्वकर्मणि

(*Thou hast a right to action, but only to action, never to its fruits; let not the fruits of thy works be thy motive, neither let there be in thee any attachment to inactivity.*)

And then,

योगस्थः कुरु कर्माणि सङ्गं त्यक्त्वा धनञ्जय
सिद्ध्यासिद्ध्योः समो भूत्वा समत्वं योग उच्यते

(Fixed in yoga, do thy actions, having abandoned attachment, having become equal in failure and success; for it is equality that is meant by yoga.)

In the very next chapter, Sri Krishna makes it clear that both Samkhya and yoga, that is jnana and karma, are equally important ways to attain the same goal.

श्री भगवानुवाच
लोकेऽस्मिन् द्विधा निष्ठा पुरा प्रोक्ता मयानघ
ज्ञान योगेन साङ्ख्यानां कर्मयोगेन योगिनां

(In this world, twofold is the self-application of the soul (by which it enters the Brahmic condition), as I state before, O sinless one: that of the Sankhyas by the yoga of knowledge, that of the yogins by the yoga of works.)

न कर्मणामनारम्भान् नैष्कर्म्यं पुरुषोश्नुते
न च संन्यसनादेव सिद्धिं समाधि गच्छति

(Neither by abstention from works does a man enjoy actionlessness, nor by mere renunciation (of works) does he attain his perfection (to siddhi, the accomplishment of the aims of his self-discipline by yoga).)

Thus, the first basic criteria for karma to become yoga is if one learns to work without any attachment to the results and harbours no dislike for any kind of work. Though it is not easy, there are certainly no shortcuts possible here; it may take years, even decades of sincere effort to accomplish this. At the initial unrefined stage of this *sadhana*, it does not matter how much work one does, or what kind of work one does, that is, whether it's for greater social good, for oneself, or for the nation. What is far more important is the attitude in which one approaches work, even if the work may appear insignificant in the overall scheme of things. It is also important to remember that like every other path, this too is a sadhana and requires time, effort and sincerity on the part of the Seeker.

Our actions in ordinary life are propelled by egoistic feelings of liking, disliking or a sense of importance. Ego is not to be understood in the limited sense of pride, but rather as attachment to anything, and it is this very attachment that leads to disappointment when things do not turn out favourably. All this is ordinary and human, nothing yogic about it. But to be able to transform ourselves such that we are neither too enthused when things go our way, nor depressed when they don't and results fail, *duhkhesvanudvignamanah sukhesu vigatasprhah*, is the true making of a yogi in action.

Once a Seeker tries to act with the attitude specified in the Gita, he develops an automatic sense of detachment; an internal division occurs where the active surface personality with all its engagements is seen as separate from the peace and detachment inside. One does not then feel that it is the individual who does the work, but rather the work is being done through him. There is no sense of possessiveness or attachment to the result, neither any disapproval for any work howsoever small or big, profitable or unprofitable as it may seem to the ordinary consciousness. Samata, equanimity in work is, therefore, the first rule of karma yoga.

Ultimately, as this detachment (not inaction) becomes settled in the consciousness, a philosophical outlook towards all actions develops within such a yogi. He becomes capable of seeing large lines of movement, of how events in the world are governed by magnificent ancient archetypal forces of various hues, who use humans as vehicles to fulfill their unique desire for play in the world of men, without having to actually incarnate here. For there is no man who has achieved something significant in the march of human history who is not an instrument of one or the other cosmic being or force, sometimes of an occult nature. Our innate egoism and the sense of appropriation make us easy instruments. We love to believe that we are the masters of our works and convictions, safely unaware of the worlds that interplay and interfere with ours. But once a karma yogi can sense what drives humans to do what they do, he automatically becomes less attached to work, and this gives him a powerful capacity for output. For whatever can be done in an excitable and agitated state of mind, can always be done better and sharper in a calmer state of being. Eventually, as this sense of philosophical detachment grows into a constant state of inner realization, the yogi develops an organic intuition about life and action, what is to be done and what is not to be done, and to what extent. This then is a kind of enlightenment in action, the state which Sri Krishna describes as seeing action in inaction and inaction in action.

कर्मण्यकर्म य: पश्येदकर्मणि च कर्म य: |
स बुद्धिमान्मनुष्येषु स युक्त: कृत्स्नकर्मकृत ||

He who in action can see inaction and can see action still continuing in cessation from works is the man of true reason and discernment among men; he is in a truly yogic state and is thus a many-sided universal worker (for the good of the world, for God in the world).

Such a man is a force in this world, for whatever he may

choose to do, or rather is driven to do, will have a long-lasting impact on this world. The Seeker then is a perfect instrument for the Divine to accomplish great tasks, which to our short-term and limited human vision may or may not make rational sense, but which, inevitably and eventually, establishes Sanatana Dharma more firmly in the world. For rationalists, this may be difficult to comprehend, but the development of a true intuition, or any such supernatural faculty, is a perfectly acceptable idea in the parlance of sadhana and spirituality of India. This, then, is real karma yoga. Not social service, good as it may be in its own merit, whether of a secular or religious nature, but action inspired and guided by the Divine so that even if such an individual were to engage in drastic and violent activities, he would not incur any sin. This is the advice Sri Krishna gives to Arjuna when the latter refuses to fight, justifying his state of sentimentalism using the logic of sin incurred in killing relatives and gurus. There is a potentially negative karmic implication in certain acts, but it is negated when we act through detachment with an evolved consciousness, irrespective of the nature and scope of the external activity.

This is the one aspect of Sanatana Dharma which has been neglected over the last few centuries, especially with great thrust on asceticism and monastic escape coupled with the general degradation of ordinary life under attacks from violent alien cultures and ideologies. Moreover, in the fight for intellectual and spiritual space against other Indic faiths like Buddhism and Jainism where a tit-for-tat karma is the fulcrum of their worldview, Hindus too digested uncritically the idea of an endless karmic give and take, making us fearful, reclusive or constrained in our actions. But this is not what the Gita told us. Pusillanimity has cloaked itself as *sattva*. We forget that the message given to the race was that of samata (equanimity) and that the yoga of karma is as important as those of jnana and bhakti, for one compliments the others. The goal is to go beyond the *trigunas*, not merely remain happy and content in *sattva*, which may be as damaging as tamas in a long enough time, and to act for the greater benefit of Sanatana Dharma—for true Dharma is not only in the transcendental *samadhis* of the world-renouncing yogis but also equally in the enlightened path of action shown by avatars like Krishna and Rama.

Of course, like any other form of yoga, karma yoga also requires tremendous inner change. To act in a far-reaching and powerful manner while being free of karmic debt is the essence of karma yoga.

An Account

A young spiritual aspirant was travelling in a remote area of the Himalayas, sometime in the first half of the twentieth century. He lost his way and ended up trapped in a hole under terrible weather conditions. Desperate and hopeless, he cried out asking why God had put him in such misery. And then he heard a voice reply, 'When you act, do you think it is you who does the work or God? And if you believed you were the originator of your actions, why blame God for your misery now?'

Decades later that youth became an enlightened yogi.

Shaktism

Among the various paths within Indian spirituality, one of the most important is Shaktism, or the worship of Shakti (Power/ Energy), which is personified as the goddess. The philosophy is known as Shaktism and an adherent of the path is called a Shakta. Some believe that this branch of spirituality originated at an ancient time from the root idea called Samkhya, which saw the world as a duality between Purusha, the male principle, and Prakriti, the female principle. While the term *prakriti* means nature in general, the term Shakti specifically denotes energy or power. Shakti always invariably involved some form of movement, for manifested energy and power is best understood through the sense of movement, while Purusha indicated a point of stillness or immobility with respect to which the movement is perceivable.

Shiva, therefore, represented the ultimate transcendental stillness while Shakti or the goddess became the sum total of all motions in the universe. The Shaktas took this idea to an extreme, proclaiming that the world as we know it is entirely Shakti. In one sense they were not wrong. Consider a simple example. At any given point the earth is in motion around the sun; the whole solar system is in motion around the centre of the galaxy; the galaxy itself is in motion around some point in the universe known as the Great Attractor and so on. Therefore, our whole existence as a species is subject to a constant play of subtle cosmic movements overlapping with each other in ways which we may not be able to understand consciously. And therefore, the Shakta scriptures proclaimed that it was the Goddess, Shakti personified, who creates, sustains and destroys this universe.

Over time, as Shaktism evolved, it practically bifurcated into two major schools—the Srikula and Kalikula. The Srikula considers Lalita Tripursundari as the main form of the goddess, while Kalikula considers Kali as the chief form of the goddess. There were other methods of classification too, based on geographical regions, but those became less prominent with the passage of time.

Tantra

Though much misunderstood and occasionally reviled, one of the most fascinating offshoots from Shaktism has been Tantra. Simplistically expressed, Tantra concerns itself with the practical application of Shakti (energy) to achieve certain desired results in the world. The more esoteric aspects of Tantra deal with the idea and practice of awakening a latent spiritual energy inside the human body, which can aid an individual's spiritual growth. This energy is traditionally referred to as Kundalini Shakti. To achieve this aim, Tantra utilizes a wide range of tools like mantras (mystical chants), *yantras* (mystical diagrams), specific visualizations along with the worship of different archetypal forms of the Divine feminine energy. The tantric texts and masters believed that the Divine is not only calm, quiet, peaceful, blissful, luminous but also powerful. Power, which is so derided in our world, is also born from the Divine. However, the only problem with power is that it can get usurped by the ego or I-sense and is thus easily misused. But the power that comes from the egoless absorption into the Divine has far-reaching potential—it can change the world, even turn an insignificant man into the effective instrument for a much greater cause. According to the Shaktas, the whole world is a projection of the power of the Divine.

Unfortunately, many people get drawn to this path for the lure of quick power and end up hastening their own downfall. Perhaps the best-suited seekers for this path are those who have transcended completely or partially their desire-motivations and ego-driven needs for control. More importantly, the tantric masters created a plethora of fantastic sadhana-related documentation about different deities and mantras and nuances of various approaches, which can prove invaluable to any sincere Seeker of any path. Many centuries after the death of the Buddha, the Mahayana sect of Buddhism developed and integrated tantric practices within their fold particularly during the reign of the Pala empire in eastern India. After the decline of Buddhism, the Baudha practices aligned with Tantra sadhana became a part of Tibetan Buddhism, which has spread across the world in the last century.

The path of Tantra, however, is impossible to traverse without a physical Guru. In theory at least one may meditate oneself into realizing the Self, but one cannot become a Tantra sadhaka without a proper Guru to guide them. There are many dangers and missteps along the path, and these can only be safely covered when a Guru handholds the Seeker. Nobody can learn Tantra sadhana from books, by second-hand methods or in any setting where the said knowledge is being disseminated en masse.

Mantra

Mantras are special words or sounds infused with a certain power, which when repeated by the *upasakas* with concentration and in accordance with the prescribed guidelines of sadhana, can bring about both material and spiritual transformation. It is believed that more than 7 crore mantras came out from the five faces of Lord Shiva. Each mantra is effectively the subtle body of the deity it invokes. Mantra sadhana has been an integral part of Dharma since the most ancient times. Traditionally, one must receive a *diksha* or initiation from a competent guru, who gives the mantra to the disciple and explains the rules of sadhana. As one practices, often doing *japa* running into lakhs of mantras, slowly a connection is formed with the devata, and a wealth of experiences happen to the sadhaka.

Siddhis

There are numerous spiritual gurus who deride siddhis. In fact, in many cases, any special effort to obtain a siddhi is considered another case of ego-enforcement and a step away from the final goal, which is only possible when the ego has been eliminated. But there are two exceptions to this. Sometimes a siddhi in the sense of a supernormal ability can come to a Seeker organically as the consciousness within changes and one moves into higher zones. There is no specific effort put towards that goal, but it happens automatically. In those circumstances, the siddhi is to be taken as a gift from the Divine and used in accordance with the Divine sanction, towards whatever end, without mixing any personal prejudice or judgement in the matter.

Siddhis can often be used as a stepping stone on the tantric path. The Guru may specifically teach the disciple a certain ability, use it to expand the disciple's consciousness, then drop that siddhi and move on. Many such great gurus can control the siddhi of a disciple, particularly a lower order siddhi, deciding when it is needed and when it must be removed. It is under the firm control of the Guru, whose guidance and experience never lets the disciple's ego take over or misuse that siddhi and thereby land up in a karmic cesspool.

Do the Shakta Texts Say Women Are Especially Divine?

Does the Shakta religion say that one must consider all women as devis? No, not really. But before one even attempts any interpretation of texts, it is mandatory to realize that the texts were written in a language known as Sandhya Bhasa, the twilight language, meaning symbolic wording, not to be taken literally. Therefore, the Guru is so important because he has the knowledge of the *parampara* to explain what things really mean. The other option is to develop one's mind by a rigorous mental exercise of objectivity over the years, but that is no easy thing. Humans in general and Indians, in particular, are exceptionally incapable of thinking without emotions. The mind in its purest form is not an instrument of emotion or even judgement, but raw, rigorous analysis leading to whatever conclusion may arise. What people normally do is first decide on the result they want by an entirely subjective and irrational process, then use the mind to lawyer up and fish for an argument to support their cause. Activism is for the sentimental being, philosophy is for the mental being—therefore, the latter has remained notoriously unpopular over ages.

What, then, is to be understood when a Shakta text says all women are goddesses? It is an attitude to be taken during the process of the mantra sadhana till siddhi, in the same vein that it recommends mantras to be done in isolated places, maintain utmost secrecy about one's practice, have perfect control over anger, eradicate lust, generally shun the company of anyone who is seen to be detrimental to the practice, and finally look at the whole world as a manifestation of the deity. It is in this context that the statement is made in Shakta texts. It does not stand as a wide dictum to be applied for all life. In fact, evidence from the lives and acts of legendary Shakta saints do not at all show they followed this. In *pramanavada*, *aptavakta* is considered an important source of evidence. In spirituality, it is, in fact, more important than literal misreading. Ramakrishna, possibly the most soft-natured of all Kali Siddhas the world has ever seen, would categorically mention that all Shakti, including women, are of two categories—*vidya* and *avidya*. The first will help you spiritually, the second will cause downfall. Don't take my word for it, read the *Kathamrita* itself. Vamakhepa, the eighteenth century ferocious Tara Siddha, would do the same when a prostitute wanted to entice him. Vama had endless siddhis! He was meditating in the cremation ground when the prostitute thought it must be fun to harass him, so she sits next to him and starts massaging his body until she felt like an electric shock that threw her away and scared the living daylight out of her. Later she gathered the courage to come and apologize. Vama, being the carefree Siddha, gave her a mantra to chant, and she eventually turned into a spiritual woman. One cannot think of Shaktas more powerful than Ramakrishna and Vamakhepa. Did they treat every individual born with an XX chromosome as a goddess? No. That defies basic common sense too, forget subtle *tattvavichara*.

There is no harm in reading texts, but there could be serious harm in reading them until one has developed one's mind. Therefore, it is imperative to find a Guru, a true Guru who shows one the path and guides one well. No man or woman is divine. They only have the 'potential' to be so, but such potential gets rarely actualized. Likewise, each of them has the potential to become perfect beasts. That this must be spelled out is a sad testimony to our general thinking (in)capacity. Without the least exaggeration, it can be claimed about very few people with confidence that their mental faculties are so well developed through conscious practice that they never let emotions disrupt logic. The key ingredient in the proper functioning of the *manomaya kosha* is objectivity. This too is a form of yoga. Unless the instrumentation of the being is in order, all practices will only breed more delusion in the mind.

PART II

Devatas

The idea of God in Hinduism is unique and nuanced. It is difficult to assign one term to specify the concept, but perhaps, as some wise men have speculated, the closest word would be 'henotheism', meaning worship of one deity while not denying the existence of other deities. The idea of many different devatas comes to us from the Vedas itself where we find Indra, Varuna, Mitra, Bhaga, Aryaman, Rudra, Vishnu, etc. In the Upanishads, which are the philosophical part of the Vedas we are unequivocally introduced to the idea of One Supreme Being, often called Brahma or Turiyam, identified with the sound of 'Om'. The word 'Turiyam' means fourth. There are three states of consciousness that a man normally experiences: his waking state, dreaming state and a deep dreamless sleep. Turiyam is what lies beyond these three, hence the fourth. Naturally, it is not only difficult to imagine, but the Upanishads are categorical that this fourth condition is entirely beyond the capacity of the normal mind to fathom.

The *Kenopanishad* states: 'The eye does not go thither, nor speech, nor the mind. We do not know It; we do not understand how anyone can teach It. It is different from the known; It is above the unknown. Thus, we have heard from the preceptors of old who taught It to us.'

The word 'teaching' here means the process of rational thinking, because if the mind does not reach there, no amount of logic and arguments can help one enter that ultimate condition of being.

So, what then are the devatas, and how do they relate to the Supreme? The word 'devata' is believed to be derived from the root '*div*', meaning 'shining' or 'celestial'. One way of looking at them is as cosmic personalities of the One who is considered the Supreme, or Ishwara. The One manifests its potential through various powerful forms, each one being unique with its own specific attributes. This idea is simple and quite common in human beings too. A man can be a father, a husband, a boss, an employee, a friend to different people yet he is uniquely the same individual. It is the same equation between the Supreme and the devatas. When the Supreme manifests as the creator, it is Brahma; as the sustainer of life it is Vishnu, and when it is the destroyer or transformer of life then he is Shiva. In the same way, Ganesha is the personality of the Supreme that removes obstacles, Durga is its power of protection and invisibility, Lakshmi is the power of harmony, Saraswati is the power of knowledge and Kali is the power to destroy evil.

The *Aitareya Upanishad* describes a man possessed by deities but governed centrally by a greater and original deity called the *atma*.

'In the beginning, this world was the Self, one alone, and there was no other being at all that blinked an eye. He thought, Let me create the world.' Then came the deities from the Self. Soon they became hungry and wanted a place where they could station themselves and 'eat'. First a cow was brought, then a horse, but both proved inadequate, so a man was created. 'The atma then told them to enter their respective dwelling (*ta abravid yathayatanam pravisata*). So, fire became speech and entered the mouth; wind became breath and entered the nostrils; the sun became sight and entered the eyes; the quarters became hearing and entered the ears; the moon became the mind and entered the heart; death became the in-breath and entered the navel.'

Finally, the atma thought these deities cannot function without it, so it pondered over which place it should enter and then decided to 'split open the head at the point where the hair part and entered through that gate' (*sa etam va simanam vidaryaitaya dwara prapadyata*).

This is a beautiful yogic description which conveys the idea that each deity is created by the Self, and though they exist externally in the cosmos at large, they also correspond to certain attributes and functionalities within man. Every entity in manifestation needs prana to survive, so do deities. This is spiritually sometimes denoted as eating, since humans get most of their pranic energy from food. So too in the case of a devata, they get their prana, akin to our food, by the concentration we direct towards them when we are engaged in their *upasana*.

Since it is very difficult for human beings to conceive of that Turiyam/Brahma/Self, therefore the greater need for Divine forms and personalities to connect to it. Do these Divine forms have an independent existence? Absolutely, they do in the world of creation, which is not only limited to human beings alone. But they are also united in the substratum called the Brahma, just like human beings and everything else in manifestation are; the only difference is that these devatas are aware of the inherent, unifying reality; humans are not. This makes the devata extremely dharmic—they never deviate from their *swadharma*, whatever that may be.

Corresponding to the idea of the Brahma is the concept of the atma inside a man. Atma is the portion of the same Divine which has created all the formidable gods and entities and universes but resides inside a human being; the rest is a biological mechanism. Therefore, the statement in Upanishads: *aham brahmasmi*, meaning I am Brahma, where the 'I' is not the normal I-sense within us or ego, but the atma, which is not yet realized in most people. So just as the atma inside of us is equivalent to the Brahma, each of our different powers, at times only present in a nascent form, correspond to the deities in the external universe. Vishnu is therefore not only a great god in the cosmos sustaining human life and Sanatana Dharma, but inside of us, he is that energy that impels us on the path of Dharma. Shiva is not only a great cosmic destroyer, but he also represents the force within man that causes change and transformation, breaking away from things, situations, conditions or people as needed. Durga is not just a tremendous devi of warfare in the universe, but she is also the force within us which gives us the power to fight when a situation so demands. Hence, the dictum of the yogis: *yatha pinde tatha Brahmande*, meaning whatever is inside us is also outside in the universe.

So, can a man realize Brahma by worship or upasana of a deity? Certainly. Because when one realizes or builds a connection one of the great devatas, he can take the Seeker into a realization of the Brahmic state too. A fitting analogy would be this: suppose there is a very complex room with many different doors through which one may enter, then each door is like a devata and the room itself is like the Turiyam or Brahma.

Each of the gods eventually inspired their own paths within Sanatana Dharma. From Vishnu came the Vaishnavas, from Shiva came Saivism, from Shakti came the Shaktas and so on. Each path has its own rules, methods and processes. While there are many differences in their methods of sadhana, all of them fit perfectly within the larger superstructure of Sanatana Dharma, and great yogis and saints have treaded all these paths to inspire people towards Dharma. One may ask what is the use of so many choices? A plethora of spiritual options exist quite simply because there are many different types of human beings and each one chooses according to their temperament. From the sweetness of Radha-Krishna to the tremendous ferocity of Rudra, no other culture has conceived of such varied notions of the Divine as Hindus. Our God is not only the delight of hearts, or a teacher to humanity as in the Gita, but he is also the terrible destroyer of things, and he also descends as an avatar when humanity needs help. An ordinary Hindu can easily worship one or more of these devatas depending on one's choice and it will never be seen as a conflict. Democracy is inbuilt in Dharma.

We are asked to build a connection with the deity we like—our *ishta devata*—through upasana, and while doing so the sadhaka is encouraged to look at that deity as the Supreme entity and consider one's life and everything in it as nothing but a play, a manifestation of that form. While trying to forge a personal relationship with the devata, one can choose from amongst the various possibilities in the spiritual texts: as a child, as a parent, a friend, as a lover, as a

Guru, and in some rare cases even as an enemy. The last equation is called Virodha Bhakti—reverse devotion, where the sadhaka hates God so intensely that he gets destroyed by God only to be saved by such a destruction. The philosophy is that the Divine is so incredibly powerful and transformative that any association with it in any capacity, even hostility, is ultimately beneficial to the Seeker. When an asura is killed by Vishnu he attains liberation. It is the same when an asura is killed by Durga in battle. The gods of Hinduism can perform terrible acts if needed, but with perfect detachment from their actions. They destroy without hatred; they love without attachment.

Sri Aurobindo wrote a beautiful prayer to the Hindu gods:

Be wide in me, O Varuna; be mighty in me, O Indra; O Sun, be very bright and luminous; O Moon, be full of charm and sweetness. Be fierce and terrible, O Rudra; be impetuous and swift, O Marut; be strong and bold, O Aryama; be voluptuous and pleasurable, O Bhaga; be tender and kind and loving and passionate, O Mitra. Be bright and revealing, O Dawn; O Night, be solemn and pregnant. O Life, be full, ready and buoyant; O Death, lead my steps from mansion to mansion. Harmonize all these, O Brahmanaspati. Let me not be subject to these gods, O Kali.

Tara

>・‥・※・‥・く

Second in the list of Mahavidyas (the first being Kali), Tara holds a special place of reverence among Tantra sadhakas both within the Hindu fold and Vajrayana Buddhists. To the latter group, this form of the goddess has ascended to a position of such ubiquitous authority that for many lay followers, Tara has become synonymous with Tibetan Buddhism. The word Tara or Tarini is derived from the root Sanskrit syllable 'tar', which means to help cross over, as in the case of crossing an ocean; in this case, it is symbolic of the ocean of *samsara*.

N. N. Bhattacharya in his work *History of the Tantric Religion* notes that the name of this goddess has apparent similarities with that of Astarte, or Ishtar, or Ashtaroth, the celebrated goddess of Akkadian Sumer Civilization in ancient Mesopotamia. Scholars like H. P. Shastri also concur on the above. As the Pala Empire fell to Islamic invaders, whose infamous iconoclasm contributed significantly to the destruction of Buddhist centres of learning, soon the remaining Baudhas left for Tibet or South Asia, and with them the centre of Tara worship also shifted to the Himalayan kingdom. However, the propagation of Tara did not stop merely with Tibet but also spread to neighbouring China, where, according to Bhattacharya, Avalokiteshwara was already on the way to being transformed from a god to goddess through the influence of the pre-Buddhist (Taoist and Confucian) goddess Si Wang-Mu. Thus, Tara completely merged with her consort, and a new deity named Kuan-Yin emerged. Through the worship of this goddess of compassion, most of the earlier Taoist rituals and beliefs became integrated with Buddhism, and this, in turn, exerted a counterinfluence onto Hindu Sakta practices through the medium of the esoteric and at times reviled path of Vamacara. It is interesting to note that the *dhyana shlokas* of the primary variants of Tara in Hinduism bear uncanny similarity with the Buddhist descriptions of Tara. Moreover, the most celebrated and revered Shaktipithas—Kamarupa, Purnagiri, Oddiyana and Jalandhara were either present near high roads leading to counties outside India or had strong cultural influence from people and worshippers of foreign origin.

It has been a subject of never-ending debate as to whether the tantric *panchatattva* rituals involving *madya* (wine), *mamsa* (meat), *matsya* (fish), mudra (parched grain), and *maithuna* (sexual intercourse) were opposed to the Dharma of Vaidika ritualism, Vedavadaviruddha, or in accordance with the spirit of the Vedic rites. Legend, as mentioned in Yamala texts like *Rudra* and *Brahma*, attests to a story, with slight variations, wherein Vashishta, the son of Brahma, practised severe austerity in Blue Mountains, Nilachala, at the site of the celebrated temple of Goddess

Kamakhya. Unable to succeed in his *sadhana* despite strenuous effort, an angry Vashishta asks Brahma for a different mantra, or he would curse this Mahavidya. Brahma stops him from uttering the curse and then describes Tara as a Supreme Shakti, who saves from all dangers, as lustrous as ten million suns, as soothing as ten million moons, dark blue (*neela*) in colour, with a brilliance surpassing ten million lightning flashes. He further says that in Her there is neither Dharma, nor Adharma, present in the form of all. She is attached to Shuddhacinacararata (pure Cinacara) as an embodiment of intelligence, *buddhishwari, buddhirupa,* and originating from the *Atharvaveda, atharvavedasakhini.*

On receiving this new advice, Vashishta then spends another thousand years in austerities with the new mantra, but he still does not succeed. Now doubly determined to curse this Mahavidya, for he is certain that this does not work, he does *acamana* by sipping water, when suddenly he hears the Devi Herself telling him that Her path is different from the Vaidika method he is pursuing. He must immediately go to *mahachhina,* where a Buddharupi Narayana will instruct him in the appropriate manner of *upasana,* which brings quick success. On reaching mahachhina, Vashishta became further agitated, so goes the story, when he sees a Buddha (not the historical Sakyamuni) indulging in the panchatattva rites, which to his unaccustomed eyes looked nothing less than perversion and outside of the Vedic *achara.* It is then that the said Buddha transforms into Narayana and the three intoxicated women surrounding him transform into the three Mahashaktis, and he enters into a colloquy with a thoroughly disturbed Vashishta, wherein he explains to the latter the real significance of these rituals and the glory of the Kulamarga, which, according to the Buddha was beyond the ordinary Vaidika ritual, Vedanamapyagocharah.

While this may come as a bit of a surprise to those who are uninitiated into tantric literature, this kind of argument is neither new nor rare. That there was a serious difference of opinion in certain class of Tantras with the Vaidika ritualism becomes clear when we find that Vedachara was considered to be the lowest, or rather the most basic kind of *achara* in the progression of upasana fit for laymen, while Kaulachara was the final sign of spiritual supremacy. Philosophically, however, there is quite a bit of similarity between the description of various spiritual states in the Upanishadic literature and tantric literature. It is in the ritual corpus that Tantra, especially the left-hand variety, marked out an independent path from the Vaidika traditions. The idea was that the Seeker must develop detachment even in those circumstances and activities which are otherwise considered impure and polluted, for one who is in the highest state of consciousness, finds everything to be filled with the essence of the Divine Shakti just as the ancient Greeks had profoundly observed, *'panta acrifi tois katharois'*—to the pure, all things are pure.

This goddess, into whose worship Rishi Vashishta was initiated, became known formally as Mahachhina Tara and eventually metamorphosed into Ugra Tara, who is accorded the high status of a Mahavidya in the Hindu tantric pantheon.

One meditation describing Mahachhina Tara goes this way:

'She stands in the pratyalidha attitude, terrifying, letting hand a garland of severed heads, dwarfish and obese, terrible, resplendent (with the colour) of the blue lotus; she has one face and three eyes; supernatural, she gives out a terrifying laughter, attahasa, while quivering with delight, she is mounted on a corpse and arrayed with eight serpents; her eyes d and round; a tiger skin clothes her hips, arrayed with five mudras,

tongue like a harpoon, all terrible, her teeth inspire fright; in her right hand she holds the sword and knife, in her left hand the blue-lotus and a skull while Akshobhya adorns her headdress. Let her be conceived in this form.'

This iconography changes in some cases with a knife instead of a sword, a burning pyre in place of a corpse, especially when the form is Shamshana Tara. According to some texts, Tara should be worshipped in a Shiva temple with an *ekalinga*, in a cremation ground, in an empty house, at crossroads, on a seat made of skulls, on a corpse, in deep water, in a battlefield, or in a lonely forest. If one is unable to visit such places, the texts recommend that the sadhaka must intensely visualize any one of these settings before embarking on the sadhana to bring about the necessary psychological condition for success in the mantra.

Another form of Tara is known as Ekjata, or one who has a single knot of hair on her head. The single *jata* on Her head is representative of an exceptional yogic focus on the state of absolute and non-dual nature of reality. She stands inside a flaming mandala, which is triangular and surrounded by a retinue of the most ferocious shaktis and servers. Those who are lazy in her practice often find themselves awakened from their lethargy by sharp pains, while those who refuse to let go of their egos, She orchestrates terrifying events that force them to transcend their I-sense and enter into the impersonal Self or state of non-duality. In Her right palm She is sometimes shown holding a blood-dripping fresh heart, ripped out from those who break their vows of Dharma. She is terrifying but She is also one of the fastest deities to confer true *adhyatma* onto a steadfast Seeker. Her mantras are kept guarded and passed onto a fit disciple from a Guru. The most interesting feature is the scissors in her hand. What is the use of meditating on a deity who holds a pair of scissors if those are not used periodically to cut off, trim away, and throw out all that is redundant, obstructive and retrograde in one's life, whether that be people, places, situations or anything else? Surely, those who devised the iconography did not do so for lazy fun but because it accurately describes what eventually is most likely to happen if the practice gains depth and power and reality.

In the setting of a shamshana to those deeply involved in sadhana, the whole world may appear one. Tara is represented by the light emanating from a funeral pyre that acts as a guide in an otherwise dark, lonely, fearsome and awe-inspiring atmosphere. Additionally, the snakes on her body are said to represent her control over the realm of *pitrs*.

As is the mechanism of deity upasanas, the sadhaka first starts meditating on the iconography of the form, which is designed to best capture the specific attributes of that devata. But eventually in the final stages, the Seeker finds a more universalized play of the devata all around until, and especially in the case of Tara, it ends in that state which is beyond description which Vedantins call Advaita and Buddhists call Shunya.

Bamakhepa, who was arguably one of the greatest Tara Siddhas known to the world, would mention during casual conversations that the highest form of Tara is the Shunya itself.

Bhairava

⟡

Bhairava holds within Himself the entire universe by reducing all the shaktis to sameness with Himself and in as much as He completely devours within Himself the entire mass of ideation which is responsible for a sense of difference .

-*Shiva Sutras*

Because Kala (Time) fears him, he is known as Kalabhairava.

Bhairava is one of the most terrifying forms of Shiva. Fear-inspiring, terrible and dreaded, except for those who are his ardent devotees. Some interpret the etymology of the terms 'Bhairava' to have been derived from the three syllables, namely '*bha*' indicating creation, '*ra*' indicating sustenance and '*va*' indicating destruction. From lore and Puranas, we get slightly different versions of the story of Bhairava's origin, but essentially it is a theme that revolves around Shiva's decapitation of Brahma's head. Once when Brahma became egotistical about his creation and declared that he is as powerful as Shiva, he has five heads exactly like Shiva does, and started challenging Shiva, the Supreme Destroyer created Bhairava from himself, who then cut off Brahma's head using the nail from the little finger in the left hand. Another version of the story says that Brahma became attached to a woman named Satarupa (in some versions like in *Shiva Purana*, Saraswati is Brahma's daughter and the object of undue attention) and kept growing heads so that he could keep an eye on her. This unholy behaviour angered Shiva and thus Bhairava was created. Whichever version of the story we take, the essential idea is that when the mind, which creates the subjective world we live in, gets hooked onto the external and develops intense attachment, that is when Bhairava strikes at the root of that ego and finishes it. No doubt he is fearful, because yogically speaking, all fear is rooted in the destruction of the ego. And death, as we define it is the most fearful of all human experiences because at that instance the ego sense which binds the mind to the physical is torn asunder and causes a tremendous shock to the organism. This too is Bhairava's domain.

But the story does not end with the mere decapitation of Brahma's head. The creator was, after all, a Brahmin, and a powerful one at that. This one act of Bhairava caused him to become the first being in the universe to commit *brahmahatya*, a grave karmic sin. To atone himself of the karmic stain, Bhairava vows to roam around as a beggar with the skull of Brahma as his begging bowl. He has an encounter with a group of sages in a Deodar Forest, who could not recognize him and only saw a dishevelled haired, skull-carrying madman, moving around, howling in joy. What caused even greater consternation to the sages was that despite his unattractive external appearance, this apparition-like figure attracted all the women in that area. Angered, they uttered a curse and his lingam fell on the ground and changed into a pillar of light. Most likely this story was told to legitimize the tantric version of Shiva worship, where the Shiva linga is not merely an aniconic symbol but symbolic of the Supreme's organ of creation. This beggar form of Shiva is known as the Bhikshatana Murti—a nude, four-armed being, surrounded by spirits and jackals, followed by lovesick women.

It must be understood that in the spiritual context, Purusha is whoever has his consciousness stationed in the Purusha tattva, and whoever does not, is a Shakti. This is more than a mere male-female concept, which means a greatly spiritual woman will have more Purusha tattva inside her than most ordinary men or women. This same concept comes to us from Vaishnavaism when Krishna is considered as the only Purusha and everyone else is but a Shakti surrounding him.

Shiva then roamed around the three worlds as a beggar, visiting different realms and various gods. When he reaches Vishnu's abode he was stopped by a gatekeeper named Vishvaksena. This angered Bhairava and he slew Vishvaksena and impaled him on his *trishula*, and carrying the corpse over his left shoulder, entered into Vishnu's domain. This act of slaying the gatekeeper added to the previous sin of brahmahatya and caused him to look like a skeleton. A new form of Bhairava emerged—Kankala Murti! In some Puranas, it is stated that Vishnu cut an artery from his own head and let that blood accumulate inside the skull-bowl, and advised Kankala Murti to visit Kashi, where he would be freed from this karma. Bhairava, who was self-intoxicated, surrounded by ghouls, spirits, dogs and jackals, carrying a corpse impaled on his trishula over his left shoulder, and a skull-bowl filled with the blood of the preserver, enters the city of Kashi. The place where his skull drops from his hand is known as Kapalamochana. From then on Kashi becomes the only place outside of cremation grounds where Bhairava resides as the guardian of the domain, granting liberation to all who die there. Again, we must not forget that India is not merely a country but a spiritual geography where different holy places occupy both physical space and an internal, psychic space. Varanasi is the city that lies between the Varuna and the Asi rivers, while Kashi is the mystical city of infinite spiritual light, whose doorkeeper is Bhairava himself. A train can take one to Varanasi, but the journey to Kashi is an inner experience!

Right from the time when Kapalikas lived in sufficient number, this great penance of Bhairava was imitated by sadhakas so that they could attain communion with him. This was known as Mahavrata, the great vow. Some scholars like Somadeva in his *Kathasaritsagar*, and Kshiraswamin (eleventh century) in his commentary on the Amarakosa lists together Mahavratin, Kapalikin, Somasiddhantin and Tantrika as adherents of the same ritual. There is even a seventh-century Chalukya grant from Nasik, which notes a donation to the Mahavratin priests of a certain Kapaleshwara Temple and an eleventh-century grant from Baroda district, mentioning a Kapalin. Of course, other mainstream sects looked at this practice with horror and ridicule and eventually as the Bhairava sadhanas became normalized and integrated, their character changed and Kapalikas became an obscure sect, almost dead. But traces of these transgressive practices became ingrained in the Tantra *marg*, especially in the dissemination known as Sabara Tantra.

In the practice of Bhairava sadhanas prevalent more in North India, he is considered as the form that Shiva assumed when he enters the drastic settings of a cremation ground. His typical offering is alcohol, and even meat; his *vahana* is a dog. A simple sign of Bhairava *siddhi* is that dogs, especially the most aggressive ones, become unusually tame and pliant to the Seeker. In due course, from Kalabhairava emerged eight other Bhairavas known as Asitanga, Ruru, Chanda, Krodhana, Unmatta, Kapala, Bheesana and Samhara. These corresponded to the *astamatrikas* of Tantra and found themselves placed in the mandala of the Devi as guardians of various realms. Another form which developed organically and probably has the maximum devotees today is a child Bhairava known as Vatuka. He is specially invoked for protection both in ritual settings as well as in secular environments. The original Nath yogis were famous for their devotion to Kalabhairava.

Bhairava sadhana, especially of the forms of Kalabhairava, when performed over long periods of time will inevitably lead one into zones which are outside of society. Probably, the reason why the Kapalika path vanished is not only because of its exclusivity and stringent requirements but also because the energy so invoked by these sadhanas make an individual progressively unfit to stay within the normal bounds of society. Bhairava is essentially a deity who stands outside of social Dharma. He leads to liberation but only for those who can give up all engagement with normal life. Psychologically he represents those clear, free, frank, and frontal movements of consciousness. The inside and the outside are in sync at all times. There is no gap, even so slight between what lies deep within, what works in the verbal flow of the mind and what comes out finally as the spoken word or performed action. His state of boundless internal freedom is represented pictorially as Shiva (stillness) residing in a shamshan (where attachments have ended), holding a skull known as Brahmanda-khappar (skull of the

Universe), drinking wine in copious amounts (a state of permanent Divine intoxication), cohabiting with women (bringing all shaktis to sameness) who come to Him willfully drawn, and other spirits, ghouls, jackals and all who are cast out of public life.

Ganesha

⟡

The devotee should meditate on Ganesha whose splendour is like the rising sun, who holds the noose and the gesture of fearlessness in his left hand and the boon-bestowing mudra and a goad in his right hand, whose face resembles that of the elephant, whose dress is red in colour, who is rendered beautiful by means of different ornaments, who is pleasing and who is extremely competent in removing all kinds of miseries.

Most ritualistic Hindu functions in this age across the world (and irrespective of the aims, secular or religious) start with an invocation of Ganesha, also known as Ganpati. Though his worship is ubiquitous today, it has been argued by scholars that the firm emergence of Ganpati as an independent and powerful remover of obstacles became a part of mainstream Hinduism around fourth–fifth century AD in the Gupta era. While coins and art figures depicting Ganpati have been recovered from as early as the Kushana period, yet the deity truly stamped his mark on the Hindu consciousness, remarkably, with the later emergence of the Ganapataya sects in western India. Even the popular story of Ganpati penning the Mahabharata is considered by some scholars to be a later addition to the great epic. The term Ganpati, though, found in the Mahabharata, is often used as an adjective for Shiva.

So, how exactly did Ganpati enter the Hindu pantheon of devatas? Some believe that the origin lies in the four or six fierce Vinayakas, whose references can be found in the *Manava-grihyasutras* and the *Yajnavalkya Smriti*. They were known as a class of dreadful troublemakers, who needed to be propitiated with various offerings, including raw meat. Eventually, these become combined into one deity, a single Vinayaka, who was appointed by Rudra as the lord of *ganas—gananam adhipataye*. The *Krishna Yajur Veda* also mentions a deity named Dantin with the head of an elephant—*hastimukha*. Of course, popular stories of Ganesha's birth are found in many of the Puranas, with slight variations, which have now become common knowledge. However, this magical transformation of a group of terror-inspiring beings into a formidable devata capable of fulfilling all human aspirations from the material to the spiritual (the *Ganpati Atharvashira* equates Ganpati with the Supreme) is something that has troubled scholars for ages. And rightly so, for the ex-post facto explanations and theories are speculative and unconvincing and seem divorced from the practical reality of present Hinduism.

Just as the iconography or symbolism of a deity is not merely the romantic fantasy of an artist, but the revealed knowledge and vision of a seer, incorporating various attributes of the devata, similarly the changes in the way a devata is perceived over time is not merely the result of a shift in societal outlook but also, equally, a transformation in the influence created by the devata himself! By the time Puranic Hinduism came into maturity, Ganpati had already become a powerful and independent God, helped no less by a family of exemplary saints who originated in northern Karnataka and eventually moved to Maharashtra near Pune. As goes the lore, this family was given a blessing that Ganesha would incarnate in their lineage for seven generations. The first among them, Moraya Gosavi, who lived during the thirteenth and fourteenth century, is undoubtedly the single-most influential factor in spreading the worship of Ganesha across western India. It is in reverence to him that Ganesha Chaturthi festivals in Maharastra are still celebrated with slogans of 'Ganpati bappa morya'. Indeed, whatever great men do, others follow. So, when certain quarters raise concerns that some aspects of worship in Hinduism have been forsaken with time, it must be reminded that this happened, at least significantly, due to the inability of those sidelined practices to produce powerful individuals, who could be emulated by masses.

As the Gita declares:

यद्यदाचरति श्रेष्ठस्तत्तदेवेतरो जनः ।
स यत्प्रमाणं कुरुते लोकस्तदनुवर्तते ॥ -Gita 3.21.

(Whatever action is performed by a great man, common men follow in his footsteps. And whatever standards he sets by exemplary acts, the world pursues it too.)

In yogic parlance, Ganesha is a personality of the Supreme that controls ganas, who are a host of occult beings acting through the agency of the physical world and can be roughly equated with the wide range of inputs received by the sense organs. Why an elephant's head? Because some believe that an elephant best represents the nature of this deity—a gentle giant in most cases, but extremely destructive when enraged. Being the Lord of ganas, he is capable of amplifying certain positive influences, while curtailing all that is troublesome to the worshipper which helps in creating a pleasant reality for the *sadhaka*. A *pouranik* verse attests to the prompt benefits that the worship of Ganesha can bring in this age—Kalau Chandi Vinayaka. In Kali Yuga, Chandi and Vinayaka bring fastest benefits. In Tantras, Ganesha is considered to be the Lord of the first chakra—*mooladhara* — and therefore capable of producing a balance between the spiritual and the material aspects of life. Naturally, unless the environment around stops drawing our awareness away into the external world, or if one is subject to constant provocations and disturbances, it is unlike that a sadhaka will be able to sufficiently concentrate his mind to enter into powerful spiritual states. At the same time, true to Hinduism's henotheistic character, Ganesha is considered the personification of the absolute Brahma for those who take him as their *ishta devata.*

Scripturally, there are at least 32 different forms of Ganesha as mentioned in the *Mudgala Purana*, most of them pertaining to specific applications with intricate mantras, rituals, and *prayogas.* Some of this knowledge was transmitted orally through various *sampradayas* in India. Though many such lines of transmission have died down, it is still heartening to see that the popularity of Ganesha worship has not shown any signs of receding. Indeed, the heart of Sanatana Dharma lies not in unquestionable dogmas and obtuse doctrines but the ability to rediscover and re-live the experiences recorded in the scriptures by every new generation. Practising religion just because it is traditional and customary is a weak argument; but if the same inherited practices or sadhanas, when performed consistently, lead to an experience of the world of gods, that automatically infuses a great vital energy in the life of the race and generates a sanguine faith on the efficacy of the traditional forms and methods of worship. May the brilliant effulgence of Ganesha illuminate our minds and invigorate our lives!

Shiva

❧❀❧

असित गिरि समं स्यात् कज्जलं सिन्धु पात्रे
सुरतरुवर शाखा लेखनी पत्रमुर्वी
लिखति यदि गृहीत्वा शारदा सर्वकालं
तदपि तव गुणानां ईश पारं न याति

*O, great master! Even, if one were to assume that the blue mountain,
the ocean, the heavenly tree, Parijata, and the earth are the ink, the
ink-pot, the pen and the paper respectively and the goddess of learning
(Saraswati) herself is the writer, she will not be able to reach the frontiers
of your greatness, however long she was to write!*

-Shiva Mahima Stotra of Gandharva Pushpadanta

Lord Shiva is one of those devatas who is equally revered in Vedic
Hinduism, the tantric path, Sabara traditions, as well as in loosely
organized folk religions of India. Shiva, meaning the 'auspicious

one', is universally regarded as one of the principal mainstream devatas in Sanatana Dharma and often associated (an association that was fixed during the pouranik age) as the destroyer among the Trimurtis or three central Divine personalities. He resides in the icy peaks of Mount Kailasa, wears a crescent moon on his head, drapes himself only in tiger or deer skin. He is the husband of Shakti, father to Kartikeya and Ganesha, has the Ganges flowing from his *jata*, holds a *trishula* and a *damaru*, and is eternally in a state of yogic samadhi. Shiva is the ultimate of all ascetics, for no being in the whole universe can match his power of *tapas*.

The first references to Shiva come from the Vedas as the terrifying, stormy figure of Rudra, probably the only one among the Vedic gods towards whom the rishis start with an attempt at pacification:

नमस्ते रुद्र मन्यव उतोत इषवे नमः
नमस्ते अस्तु धन्वने बाहुभ्यामुतते नमः

(*Salutations to your Ire, Rudra and also salutations to your arrow*
Salutations to your bow and also to both your arms.)

Shiva's bluethroat, Neelakantha, is evidence of His power to consume and transform just about anything, including the most *tamasic* of substances like the poison of the whole world, Halahala. Consequently, there is a tradition of offering things like Dhatura (which can be quite poisonous) to Lord Shiva. Shiva is always shown in a state of deep *samadhi*, a self-intoxication; only this is different from normal human condition of samadhi where the world gets negated, because in Shiva's samadhi He is aware of Himself so deeply that he becomes aware of everything around in the Universe, because ultimately His own Shakti or consciousness has created the Universe. In recognition of this Divine intoxication, there is the tradition of offering bhang or other intoxicants to Lord Shiva.

Shiva is shown wearing a scanty tiger or deer skin, sitting almost naked in the coldest peak of Kailasa. He is thus the lord of *tapasya*, of penance, for no being in the Universe, deva or asura, can match his capacity for austerity. That too he can grant to a devotee if the latter so desires and is able to draw Shiva's grace towards himself or herself. It is interesting to note that in the Mahabharata, Mahadeva is perhaps the most worshipped of gods. Even Krishna had done tapas for Shiva, which resulted in his son Samba, among other benedictions.

Shiva is always associated with liminal conditions, heterodox spaces, particularly the charnel grounds. In Tantra, he is shown to reside in the head inside the thousand-petalled lotus, which is as beyond as it is possible for a human being or society to imagine. Of the One Supreme Reality, Shiva represents its purely transcendental persona, He who stands apart and watches, and has no favourites or takes no sides in anything or anywhere in creation. Humans are but one aspect of creation. His impartial transcendent power is experienced even among the non-human residents of the Universe like Gandharvas, Yakshas, *bhutas*, *pretas*, Nagas, etc. Therefore, anyone who can appease Shiva, can get any boon from him—a fact that asuras have used numerous times to their benefit, as mentioned in the Puranas. In his eyes none of them are better or worst, special or inferior. This fact is further demonstrated when Shiva is shown surrounded by hordes of *ganas*, so odd and terrifying that the whole group can be classified as outcasts from the human society and consciousness. Auspicious and inauspicious is transcended, good and bad are brought to sameness in Shiva's supreme consciousness. In His eyes all are but an expansion of His own Shakti. This also makes him, in human parlance, gullible or *bhola*. Hence, the name Bholenath. It is this superhuman, unthinkable detachment from Creation that makes Him have such infinite power over Creation. If the world of Creation is a hurricane, Shiva is the eye of that hurricane, the point of maximum stillness where not a blade of grass will move. It is why the earliest and best representation of Shiva is the structure of the Shiva linga—steady, unshakable, undisturbed by anything around.

This has also easily made him Parameshwara, the Supreme Lord, in the Vedantic schools of non-duality. That which is beyond the mind (and therefore beyond Creation) but resides deep inside the *hridaya guha* (a term used in Upanishads), the cavity of the heart, which when experienced obliterates the division between the *kshetra* and the *kshetrajna*, the field and the knower of the field of knowledge. Thus, the knower, the known and the process of knowledge become one. This is the Absolute Himalaya of non-duality, Advaita. And this is the state of Shiva where He becomes the Supreme Self—'I' beyond the eye.

We also get the story of Shiva's destruction of Daksha's *yajna*. Daksha means the one who is an expert. The purpose of this tale is that one who has attained a perfection of ritualism (like Daksha) but refuses to entertain the Divine (Shiva) in his mental schema, believing falsely that by mere exceptional ritual performance he may attain to whatever goal he so desires is destined to be decimated and is nothing more than an animal known for its universal stupidity in occult literature; the goat, whose head is planted on Daksha after Shiva decapitates him. This brings about the most vital idea that has become ingrained in the various Shaiva paths, that even simple acts of devotion, with or without sufficient scriptural knowledge can still evoke the compassion of the God of gods.

Mahashivaratri on the *chaturdasi tithi* of Phalgun *masa* is almost universally regarded as a great occasion for worship, meditation, asceticism and devotion to Lord Shiva. The significance of it is referred to in various Puranas like the *Skanda, Linga, Padma, Shiva,* etc. Some believe that this was the night when Shiva performed his cosmic dance of creation and dissolution known as the *tandava nritya*, while other traditions, particularly the Shaktas believe this was the night when Shiva was married to Shakti.

Spiritually, both these two background stories of Lord Shiva point to the same idea—only when the Purusha tattva joins with Shakti, that creation (which is desirable) is enabled and that is what Shiva's dance also embodies—cycles of constant creation and destruction like the endless flow of water in a river. Every moment things change only to create something new.

This makes Mahashivratri auspicious for all devotees of Shiva and Shakti. In fact, by most accounts, this is arguably the holiest night where any kind of spiritual effort may be blessed by the grace of Shiva to fruition. From Vedic to Pasupatas, Aghora, Sabara, to tantric, almost every tradition places Shiva on a pedestal of great reverence, for even an ounce of Shiva tattva inside an individual makes them capable of breezing over the difficult waters of existence blissfully—safe, secure, and unharmed. The great God of gods, Mahadeva, may or may not change one's destiny, but he can show the Seeker how to remain unaffected by things around while enjoying the bliss of self-intoxication. And that is a prize worth lifetimes of effort!

Hanuman

◦◦◦

The Valmiki Ramayana describes Hanuman as a *mahapandita* (great scholar), *mahavira* (of tremendous valour), a master of Vedas and Vedanga. He is also described later as Bajrang, one who has a body as strong as lightning. By the tenth century, Hanuman was regarded as an *amsha* of Shiva and this association is reflected in many popular prayers to Hanuman like the Hanuman Chalisa. In Maharashtra, Sri Ramdas, who was Shivaji's Guru, composed many beautiful stotras to Hanuman, of which the Bhimarupi Maharudra is particularly popular.

The strength of Hanuman has always been awe-inspiring, and often invoked for protection from any kind of evil, while his Dasabhava, servility to Sri Rama, is a fine example of how the human soul must submit to the power of the Supreme, thus transforming itself from a limited animal, a monkey, to the supremely powerful Hanuman.

Panchamukhi Hanuman has been regarded as one of the most powerful secondary emanations from a major deity, whose power, strength and Shakti manifest itself through the *panchatattva* (hence five faces) and overcomes all obstacles regarding the same. Aghori Sri Vimalananda, whose biography was published by his disciple in Aghora series of books, describes his sadhana of Panchamukhi Hanuman in the cremation grounds. As the *sadhana* slowly reaches its pinnacle, a lightning strikes with earsplitting thunderclaps around the *sadhaka*, each time getting scarily close to where he was seated. For an unprepared nervous system, communion with a ferocious deity is not only unlikely but such attempts are foolish and dangerous. That, however, does not mean ordinary worship of deities, even those who are extremely *ugra* cannot be done; some merit surely comes through the route of sincere faith and *upasana*. What however does not come by this method is *siddhi* or communion with the devata, for it needs apt methods and guidance. It is here that the Guru becomes vital because only a competent authority can decide which form of which deity is the best fit for an individual sadhaka.

Kali

From the knitted brows of her forehead's surface immediately came forth Kali, with her dreadful face, carrying a sword and noose. She carried a strange skull-topped staff and wore a garland of human heads. She was shrouded in tiger skin and looked utterly gruesome with her emaciated skin. Her widely gaping mouth, terrified with its lolling tongue, sunken, reddened eyes and a mouth that filled the directions with roars. She fell upon the great asuras in that army, slaying them immediately. She then devoured the forces of the enemies of the gods, attacking both the front and rear guard, having seized the elephants. Together with their riders and bells, she hurled them into her mouth with a single hand. Likewise, having flung the cavalry with its horses and the chariots with their charioteers into her mouth, she brutally pulverized them with her teeth. She seized one by the hair and another by the throat. Having attacked one with her foot, she crushed another against her breast. The weapons and missiles that were hurled by the demons, she seized with

her mouth and crunched them to bits with her teeth. She destroyed the
army of all those mighty and distinguished demons. She devoured some
and thrashed the others. Some were sliced by her sword, others pounded
with her skull-topped staff.

- *From the Devi Mahatmyam,*
Chapter 7. Translation by Coburn

Kali is one goddess who has always evoked a strange mixture
of divinity and terror, especially among those uninitiated or
unaccustomed to her peculiar ways. However, for the Hindu seers,
who were not conditioned to look at Reality in only its sweet and
joyous aspects but also the terrifying and destructive forms, Kali is
both a ferocious destroyer of asuric forces, and a mother to those
who worship her. Historically, one particular categorization of
the Shaktas was based on geography, wherein the Northeastern
portion was known as Vishnukranta, and this is where the worship
of Kali reached the highest prominence.

Kalikula or the lineage of Kali, as it is more commonly known by
its followers, is a complex blend of philosophy and ritual with Kali
residing at the fulcrum of the path and auxiliary deities considered
as emanations of Kali. Noted Indologist N. Bhattacharyya writes,
'The followers of Kalikula are exclusively monists. They hold
Shakti as the same as Brahma in its three aspects of *sat* (reality),
chit (consciousness) and *ananda* (bliss), and not its *mayavivarta* or
transformative aspect.'

Scholars believe that the earliest texts pertaining to
Kalikula may have been lost. Kalikula was in inception related
to the Uttaramnaya categorization of paths, created from the
superstructure of Atimarga-Kapalika practices as a sixth and more
powerful transmission beyond the five sources of Saiva traditions.

In certain old texts of this school, we find mentions of a goddess named Kalasamkarsini, who is believed to have transformed into Kali at a later period. Perhaps the oldest manuscript on Kali worship preserved today is the *Yonigahvara* dated approximately at 1200 AD. It forms part of a larger text on Chandabhairava, which emerged from the ancient Shaktipitha of Oddiyana. The setting of the contents is in the cremation ground of Oddiyana, where Bhairava, surrounded by yoginis, speaking to his consort describes Kali as 'beyond the senses, inconceivable, of free volition, free from defects, identical with the stainless supreme sky, free from desires, residing in the sphere beyond the firmament'. It then speaks of the lineage of gurus who were adept in this vidya and mentions Minanatha as the chief exponent of this yuga. Beyond the rituals and procedures associated with this path, it also mentions the various divisions, *bhedas* of Kali, and how they eventually merge into the rare and powerful, or transcendental form of Guhya Kali.

The tantric initiate who sought to follow the path of the Kalikula basically aimed at incinerating his limitations or *pasas* through a combination of unpredictable, terror-inducing, heterodox and intensely transgressive rituals executed with the attitude of a hero—*virabhava*. The term '*vira*' here needs more elucidation. While it normally means brave, in tantric literature, it further denotes the second of the three categories into which all sadhakas are differentiated, that is, one who has gone beyond a herd-mentality-driven life of a *pashu*, and turned himself into a vira, who courageously and willfully works out his own spiritual salvation against any odds that life may throw up, but has not yet reached the level of the *divya* or Divine. Some read it as another subtle way of putting the caliber of a sadhaka into perspective. A pashu is a gross literalist, who can only understand what his five senses allow him to, while the vira is one whose intelligence has become more subtle and therefore is capable of accessing the *adhidaivika jagat* or the astral world. The divya is beyond even this and has entered into the *adhyatmika jagat*; he is in constant communion with the Brahma (here Shakti), therefore not bound by any rules, or whatever he may do is a rule in itself. While there are many severe restrictions mentioned for the pashu. For example, he should not worship at night. The main corpus of the tantric texts was designed to act as guides for the *vira sadhaka*.

One of the predominant features of the initial style of Kalikula is *vira sadhanas*, which is followed even today, but in reduced volume, involving ritualized engagement with objects from a cremation ground and use of items prohibited in standard religious practice. The initiated vira is supposed to meditate on Kali, or one of her emanations, inside a *shamshan* on specific *tithis* like *ashtami, chaturdasi* or *amavasya*, while consuming ritually consecrated alcohol known as *karana* accompanied by one's partner called *bhairavi*. In other instances, a group of sadhakas may form an occult circle of worship called *chakrapuja* in appropriate settings to harness a greater collective power of invoking Kali. Naturally, such heterodoxy was deemed severely offensive to mainstream religious sensibilities. Therefore, Shakta Tantra developed on the fringes of the society, often keeping its practical secrets of sadhana and philosophy notoriously guarded against the masses. An oft-repeated saying demonstrated the attitude adopted by the viras:

अन्तः शाक्तः बहिःशैव सभायां वैष्णव मतः
नाना रुपधराः कौलः विचरन्ति महीतले

(At heart a Shakta, outwardly a Shaiva, in gatherings a Vaishnava, in thus many a guise the Kaulas wander on earth.)

To the unaccustomed mind, these may seem dangerously random acts of willful divergence from the mainstream, but it had its own logic and schema. Moreover, while a lot of freedoms were allowed to the individual sadhaka of this path based on his own strengths and weaknesses, there was still a broad and sound overarching structure in place that guided the individual. For example, in practice, vira sadhanas had a *krama* or progression into realms of greater complexity that was adhered to by specific sampradayas. One such krama that was popular till the nineteenth century in a sampradaya centred around an ancient and famous Shaktipitha, the sadhaka was required to first complete his *vira siddhi*, that is, establish himself as a vira. This would entail a series of cremation ground rituals designed to take the Seeker beyond fear, shame and disgust. After the Guru ratified the vira, he would then go onto perform Dakini sadhana. Dakini in Hindu Tantra is considered to be an extremely malevolent spirit, more dangerous than the regular *bhuta* and *preta*. The practice was considered so risky that the Guru would often assign an *uttarasadhaka*, an accomplished Tantra sadhaka, to act as an aid and protector for the vira. When the sadhaka would sit inside the ritual setting in some desolate region away from locality, inside a forest or a cremation ground, on a *mundasana* chanting appropriate mantras, the uttarasadhaka's job was to maintain the *kilana*—the protective circle around the sadhaka and chant mantras for his protection. Old texts from eastern and northern India in local languages mention that this particular sadhana was so dangerous that the slightest error or lack of nerves would leave the Seeker mad or suicidal. Thus, there could be no halfway measures, no second chances. The author has witnessed the devastating effects that such methods can have on those who are psychologically unfit, yet attempt these sadhanas out of false bravado, or overestimation of one's capabilities. Given the extreme nature of this process, for every individual who succeeded, there would be many, who were reduced to a complete wreck.

When this too had been accomplished, then and only then the sadhaka in this *sadhanakrama*, was considered fit to worship the Mahavidya Kali. It is important to note that as such anybody can worship a deity. It is however an entirely different matter for the worship to reach a level wherein the deity also responds to the call. Very few achieve this two-way communion. To make one capable of reaching that level of psychological fitness and develop the necessary subtlety of mind and senses, such that the deity, in this case Kali, responds, and one is able to understand the response, that this kind of a krama was designed for the initiated Tantra sadhakas of this sampradaya. For in the Shakta philosophy, worship without palpable results, based on unverifiable claims of next-worldly goodies or merely conforming to tradition, is not enough. One must experience and then demonstrate that experience, or if so capable, transmit it to those, who may have the *adhikara* for it. Quite often, therefore, one finds that two sadhakas performing the same ritual will have nuanced variations while following a broad ritual superstructure. These nuances develop with time and practice, according to the specific needs and capabilities of every individual sadhaka. And this is where Vedic ritualism differs from tantric ritualism. In the former, exact performance of the ritual is given primacy and the reward is metaphysical, while the latter places a greater premium on results, which must be demonstrated immediately, or within a short time.

When an amavasya coincides with a Saturday, then it's ideal for placating disturbing *pitrs*, mollifying Saturn, or doing upasana of Kali.

As the last yuga deepens, and asuric forces become more and more powerful, Kali becomes the most prominent and active among devatas who participate in the world of humans. Her unstoppable power decimates asuras. Even a little of Her grace is sufficient to protect a Seeker in any astral plane against any kind of entity or attacks.

कलौ काली कलौ काली कलौ काली वरप्रदा
कलौ काली कलौ काली कलौ काली तु केवला

Agni

❦

अग्निमीळे पुरोहितम् यज्ञस्य देवं ऋत्विजं
होतारं रत्नधातामं

(I worship the Fire God, who is the divine priest of the ritual of the sacrifice, who bestows excellence.)

-*Rig Veda*

It can be assumed that the first instances when early humans interacted with fire must have been from lightning strikes, or by observing the remnants of some half-burnt tree or shrub in the wilderness. Then, at least 1.9 million years ago, hominids started controlling fire, though it became widespread only around 1,00,000 years ago. One of the earliest known evidence of the controlled use of fire comes from Gesher Benot Ya'aqov, Israel, about 7,90,000 years ago. This single act of controlling fire, no doubt, caused a vast evolutionary and cultural change in our behaviour, health and energy expenditure. Not only that, it also gave us a new way of looking at the world around, a supremacy which probably did not exist in an ancient era driven by predatory forces and drives. While the animal kingdom is physically apt, agile and better suited than humans to survive in the wild, they all have an instinctive fear of fire. Important too is the fact that the art of cooking food caused our bodies to absorb more nutrients, resulting, eventually, in a shrinking of the long intestine and a rapid expansion of the brain and its capabilities, which otherwise, may not have been possible. In short, it would not be an exaggeration to say that fire humanized us!

But agni is not merely a natural process, a study in combustion, but also an integral part of most Indo-European religious thought. He is regarded verily a God in his own right! The *Rig Veda* starts with a hymn to agni, calling on fire to act as the first priest, the officiator of the Vedic sacrificial rituals and the one who brings the devas to our realm. Since at least the Treta Yuga, when Lord Rama was supposed to have lived, fire has been an integral part of rituals for Sanatana Dharma. Not just in Hinduism, evidence suggests that most ancient cultures are known to have revered fire in some manner or the other as a symbol of the Divine, and its power of burning and illumination was used for making ritual offerings to other deities. While Zoroastrians are known for their fire worship and fire temples, the Graeco-Roman tradition had deities connected to fire like the Greek Vesta and the Roman Vulcan. The Titan Prometheus, in Greek mythology, is supposed to have stolen fire from the gods and gifted it to humans. In Celtic mythology, Belenus is connected to fire, as was Svarog, (cognate of the Sanskrit word *swarga*) of Slavic religions. Even the earliest

Semitic texts contain references to fire sacrifices performed by prophetic figures like Noah. The word 'holocaust' from Greek Holokautein (ὀλοκαυτεῖν) in its pristine sense refers to a complete and thorough sacrifice of fire where no remnants of the original offerings are left behind.

Agni in Hinduism

The Vedic fire rituals were grand, elaborate affairs often involving mass community participation as well as individualistic efforts. These were known as *yajna* and played a great role in the *karmakandic* or ritualistic worship preferred by the Mimamsaka school and its adherents. Complex, geometrical fire alters were created, strict rules for offering were made, and rishis conducted these ceremonial yajnas for the overall material and spiritual benefit of the whole community. Over time, the term yajna came to mean any kind of sacrifice or offering, and eventually spreading out into the five forms—*bhuta yajna, manushya yajna, pitr yajna, deva yajna, brahma yajna*—but in the historical context it was primarily an offering through fire.

As yajnas became less frequent, *homas* (from the root *'hu'*, meaning 'offering into a fire') became more popular. These are much small-scale fire rituals that can be performed by individuals, either with specific aims or for general spiritual progress. Historians say that evidence of homa-like rituals can be found across Asia from ancient Samarkand to Japan for at least 3,000 years. Philosophically there are two distinct ways in which fire is regarded as a medium of worship in Indo-European religions. First, as a vehicle of sending our oblations to the realm of the gods while bringing down gifts and benedictions from them. Secondly, agni is one of the five great elements of creation, with the special attribute to swiftly invoke the energies of the other divine beings within because it is extremely pure. Hence, one of the ancient names for agni is *pavaka*. Thus, a homa involves a *pranapratisthapana* of the deity inside the flames of agni using appropriate mantras and mudras and then making offerings to the deity. It must be remembered that the basic idea of worship and *sadhana* is always to use one of the five main constituent elements—*prithvi, jal, agni, vayu* and *akasha*— as the conduit or medium through which the Shakti of the deva is to be accessed. So, when a murti is worshipped, it is akin to using the *prithvi tattva* to approach the devata, while a homa uses the agni *tattva*.

Each of these tattvas has specific attributes which need to be kept in mind while using them. For example, the prithvi tattva is slow and steady. Therefore, to infuse Shakti into an idol may take years of worship. Whereas agni is fast and transformative, that is, it can turn any substance into ash. This quality makes worship through agni produce quicker results. Anyone who has performed fire rituals for sufficient time will notice that agni can cause a subtle vitalization of thoughts and in effect, the mantras being chanted near the fire result in a deeper resonance inside the consciousness of the individual. This ability of agni has tremendous significance in spiritual practices. Further, the smell from the burnt offerings causes an astral purification of the area, where homas are regularly performed. There is no magic here but only a process and the realization that comes through consistent practice and observation. Not so long ago, fire rituals were a regular part of Hindu households. Even Naga sadhus, a branch from within the ascetic sects of Hinduism, while renouncing everything else, including clothes, still maintain their *dhunis*—constantly burning fires, where they perform regular worship.

Agni as Other Devatas

The chief attribute of agni which makes it a potent internal symbol as well as an external deity is its ability to transform everything, purifying all that is added onto it and bringing them to sameness, the ash, or *vibhuti*. Its constant upward face while burning is considered to be a sign of righteousness, a single pointed focus on the realm of the devas. There are, in fact, some other popular deities in Hinduism who are believed to have a link to agni. For example, the southern face of Shiva, known as Aghora—that which is non-terrifying—is linked to agni. It could also be due to the swift and dreadful nature of this path that it has been linked to fire. Among the avatars of Vishnu, the man-lion form of Narasimha has clearly an unmistakable link to fire. It may be apt to recall here Sri Aurobindo's commentary on the ten principal avatars and the progress of consciousness across various life forms on earth for more effective and varied self-expression. Narasimha represents the stage where consciousness progresses from the animal forms into the human. Hence, the symbolism of transition surrounding the story of this avatar. He was neither animal nor man, appearing in the interlude between day and night, from an object that is so simple and unexpected—a pillar. As if an intense and powerful force erupted out of the normal status quo of animal life and gave birth to another level of consciousness which needed a newer and more capable *adhara*, a human being. What could this be if not fire, which when introduced into the world of hominids, produced such a quick and tremendous evolutionary progress?

The Agni Within

The red-glowing mass of him is seen: a great god has been delivered out of the darkness.

Rig Veda V.1.2

Sri Aurobindo in his writings on the psychic being, or 'chaitya purusha', makes a brilliant connection that the fire's inner symbolism, apart from its function in external worship, relates to the birth of the spiritual aspiration in the depth of one's heart, without which no progress is ever possible. Indeed, only those who have this fire in them will probably move towards a greater expansion of the *chitshakti*, despite many difficulties and obstacles, which are anathema to spiritual life. In this sense too, agni acts as the priest officiating between the human world and the realm of aspiration of the devas. In yogic parlance, a human being has at least two different kinds of agni inside him—the *jatharagni*, which digests food, and the *bhutagni*, which digests intellectual matter. Both cannot be equally active simultaneously. When great concentration is applied to any subject—spiritual or secular, it increases the bhutagni in the individual thus reducing hunger in the physical body. The importance of this intellectual fire cannot be overstated, for, without this, no amount of spiritual practice bears tangible results. One may perform various complex sadhanas, but one will have no ability to digest the results of those and integrate them into his waking consciousness unless this agni is burning bright inside one's mind and subtle body. Consequently, a constant and powerful bhutagni will reflect in the personality as an increase in *tejas, ojas* and subtle prana, a greater life force and a resplendent intellect. Ayurveda further subdivides this bhutagni again into five divisions corresponding to the five fundamental elements, while clearly describing its overall aim to metamorphose and subsequently absorb into the mind-body complex all that is needed for growth and development, both material and spiritual. On the other hand, a vitiated inner agni results in an imbalanced metabolism, showing an increase in *pitta*, one of the three primary doshas in Ayurveda. It is interesting to note that in the Greek story of Prometheus, the punishment meted out to him by Zeus for stealing the fire of gods was that he would be chained to a rock where his liver is eaten daily by an eagle, only to be regenerated at night due to his immortality. Now any basic text of Ayurveda will tell us that the source of pitta in the human body is the liver. Maybe this myth was a way of conveying the truth that misusing the fire element inside the body can lead to a regular aggravation of pitta in daily life, which of course can get pacified by a good night's sleep.

However, the greatest inner spiritual manifestation of the fire is the coiled up evolutionary force in the human mind-body, known to tantric yogis as the Kundalini Shakti. Having the nature of fire, it marks an upward journey of metamorphosis, transforming the animal within to the human and the human to the Divine, eventually. Even a regular simplified worship through the medium of agni purifies both the inner and the outer atmosphere around such a sadhaka. Negatives are stopped or their intensity reduced, positives are enhanced, and the blessings of the gods are brought forth into one's life. The shastras describe a constant war between the devas and the asuras in the various non-physical realms, which spill over into our world in the form of drastic and painful events. In this battle between Light and Darkness, the regular and consistent worship of fire acts as a significant boost, an invitation to the Divine forces to participate in the world of mortals and tip the scales of this endless war in favour of all that adheres to Dharma and *satya*. It was not for nothing that the ancient rishis would conduct such elaborate fire rituals on a regular basis!

Having performed regular homas for a decade to various deities as an act of individual sadhana and having interacted with other sincere seekers who perform similar spiritual practices, this author can vouch for the powerful consciousness-altering capacity of agni rituals. The *Rig Veda* uses an epithet for agni—Jata Veda, one who knows all things. But what does it really mean? To find out, one must build a relationship with agni and let its radiant might infuse the Seeker's mind, for some things are better experienced than read.

Kubjika

She is a rare and secret tantric form of Shakti, whose liturgy and esoteric details were brought out into the world of scholarly examination and general public eye by scholar Mark Dyczkowski. Scholars believe that Kubjika was originally a part of the Kashmiri tradition in another name and from there, this *vidya* was transmitted probably by the influence of the Nath yogis like Matsyendra towards Nepal. There is also a view that the Kubjika Mata had multiple streams, of which most have faded today, and some of them have references to gurus older than the Naths, who were only channels of transmission. However, as per the Kubjikamata Tantra, today this vidya is universally regarded as pertaining to the *paschimamnaya*. The term 'amnaya' is used to denote distinct groups of scriptures within the Kaula Agamas that share a common affiliation to a single tradition and originated from or propagated towards a fixed direction. There are five such amnayas, four in the cardinal directions and one upwards. Sometimes these are also equated with the five vital breaths inside a human being. Paschimamnaya refers to the western direction, which is synonymous with the *vyana vayu*, and it is in this tradition that Devi Kubjika's *shasana* is unquestionable.

The Newars, particularly the kings of the Malla dynasty and their priests were all believed to have worshiped Devi Kubjika as a tutelary deity and it was around them that a thriving cult of Kubjika *upasakas* survived in Nepal since the twelfth century, while the goddess had almost been forgotten in the land of her origin. However, no official temple of Kubjika was ever created, neither is she as well-known as some of the other tantric forms of Devi like Kali. Utmost secrecy was a paramount feature of Kubjika Mata. There is a story passed down orally that a certain prince of the Malla dynasty had violated the modesty of a young girl, whose father was an exalted devotee of the goddess, and this defilement incurred the wrath of Devi Kubjika on the royal family. She removed her protection, and the line of Mallas came to an end when Prithvi Narayan Shah of the Gorkha Kingdom invaded Kathmandu in 1768–1769 CE at the Battle of Kirtipur.

Iconography

Like in most forms of Shakta puja, it is believed that Devi Kubjika had different iconographies according to the specific nature of her emanation and its propagation in a particular cultural setting. One of her earliest forms, as depicted in the texts, describes her with six faces, worshipped along with a Panchamukhi Mahadeva and her body is adorned by Nagas: Karotaka as a waistband, Takshaka as an ornament between her chest and waist, Vasuki as a garland, Kulika as her earrings. In her hands, she holds a skull, a king-cobra, a crystal-bead rosary, khatvanga (skull-topped rod), *sankha*, book, *trishula*, mirror, *khadga*, a necklace of rare gems, *ankusha*, and a bow. Her complexion is like that of a Kunda flower. In another form where she is known as Vakreshvari, her six faces are known as Para, Malini, Matrika, Kalika, Tripura, and Khechari.

The word Kubjika in Sanskrit means hunchbacked. Mark Dyczkowski describes in his tome that she is also known as Kubji, Kuja, Kuji, Khanjini—the Lame One; Vakrika or Vakra—the Crooked One; Cincini—the goddess residing in the Tamarind tree; Kulalika—the Potteress; Amba or the vernacular forms as Avva, Anama, Laghvika and most common of all as Sri—the Royal One. Her nature is best described as a secret among secrets—*guhyati guhya*, and her influence on royalty is well attested by the manner in which the Newar Royal family had a close association with her, and yet her *upasana* remained hidden from the masses. Only the initiates passed it on from one generation to the next. But why is she called crooked? Probably of all feminine Divine forms in Hinduism, Devi Kubjika is the clearest personification of the human ego or *aham*, which controls our very existence and creates the sense of individualization. What is aham in a normal human being, is also the 'sleeping' or unawakened state of this Kundalini Shakti—that residual supernatural force which lies dormant inside the human body and can be activated by serious yogic/tantric practices. Once awakened in a controlled manner, this Shakti accelerates an individual's spiritual evolution at a breakneck speed. Therefore, the paths that required utilizing the force of Kundalini were always extremely Gurumukhi because just as a powerful Kundalini awakening can take an individual into a completely different sense of reality, same way the smallest of mistakes can derail the Seeker and keep him trapped in a well of delusion, or worse throw him down into a miserable condition far worse than what he had initially started from. This tremendous Shakti was revered, respected and treated with adequate caution among the initiates. A fully awakened Kundalini shoots upwards and merges in the Akula—one who is beyond the Kula or Shiva, while during ordinary conditions she stays right inside the body but perfectly hidden from our normal awareness. After all, no human being is aware of his own I-sense rather aham when he goes about his daily ordinary functions, yet without the aham, there would be no individual in the first place. This phenomenon of being all-pervasive yet perfectly hidden in the background is also the core nature of Kubjika.

A story goes that once Shiva came to hold her hand, but the Devi was unsure and reticent for a moment. In that state of hesitation she became hunched. That is how Kubjika or Vakreshwari came into existence. Spiritually, Shiva represents the ultimate Divine state, but this consciousness cannot enter or reside inside our fragmented, ignorant selves, which we are in the normal condition.

That is why the concept of *tattvashuddhi* or *adharashuddhi* is very important. Adhara simply means the receptacle—mind and body. Until they are purified, they cannot hold the Divine inside. This same idea also comes to us from the Ramayana when Ravana decides to bring Kailasa to Lanka. Kailasa is the physical representation of the higher consciousness of Sahashradala where Shiva or the Divine resides. Lanka is the *mooladhara*, which governs the physical existence of our five senses and roots us to the earth.

A great purification of the mooladhara can bring tremendous material riches and benefits, just as the descriptions of Lanka noted how the kingdom was flooded with gold and material opulence. But the standard spiritual path is for the Shakti to rise from mooladhara and finally reach Kailasa, not the other way round, and certainly never an absurd cohabitation of the Divine with the limitations of the lower chakra. Naturally, Ravana met with disaster when Shiva pressed his foot on to the Rakshasa Lord's hands and pinned him down for a thousand years! In the same way, the aham that works in our ordinary life cannot suddenly give up its ignorant ways and turn itself over to self-annihilation and submit to the Divine. An ordinary man, if he were suddenly to encounter an experience of an otherworldly nature, would first be rattled, and then use his mentality to justify what may be incorrect about it, or labour under stressful thoughts of why a spiritual turn may not be right at this moment, given that such may hamper with whatever worldly Dharma he is currently engaged in. Valid or invalid, this is exactly how the aham works. It will never ever willfully sign its own death warrant, and it knows exactly how to convince the mind and emotions to choose a solution where its control over the individual remains untarnished. This is why Kubjika Shakti hunched herself backward and earned the epithet Vakra, when Shiva came to hold her hand, for this is the most natural human reaction when faced with something extraordinarily beyond our mental conceptions. But that is only the beginning when the real journey has not yet started. By upasana of this form, eventually, the Seeker experiences how Kubjika, the unremarkable hunchbacked lady, suddenly starts straightening and shooting upwards, piercing through the chakras and changing the Seeker's subjective experience of the world around until she merges into Akula. Whenever there is someone who experiences the effects of a Kundalini *jagran*, irrespective of the path, time, place or culture, it's always by her sanction alone that it must transpire, even if the individual may have never heard of Kubjika Devi.

When fashioning this delicate and transformative journey, the Seeker is forced to undergo changes in his mind and emotions, his daily routine and interactions in order to safely sustain the power rushing through his body. The human adhara is like raw clay, and Kubjika creates the pot that can bear her strength and power sustainably. Thus, she is called Kulalika, the Potteress. Additionally, when Kubjika passes beyond the Manipura chakra she starts manifesting her powers most visibly, and the first is an unmistakable lordliness in the Seeker. Kubjika is therefore also known as Sri—the Royal One. In Tantra sadhana, every path has a Kulavriksha, a tree that represents the Devata. For Kubjika Mata it is the tamarind tree.

The nine great Nath yogis were believed to be worshippers of Kubjika and it is through them that the upasana of this form spread across India, even to the South. Now, of course, the Devi is neither remembered, except perhaps in some esoteric circles, nor do we find any temples dedicated to her. Coming across a Kubjika sadhaka is extremely rare. The secrecy involved in this sadhana ensured that while Kubjika was highly revered and equally feared, she was never a deity for the public. Even in places where a strong cult of traditional Kubjika upasakas kept the vidya alive, we find almost no trace of temples or public festivities associated with her. A good reflection of the fact that even when theoretical knowledge about Kundalini is only a click away on Google, the real experience is still highly unusual, extremely rare and defies set formats or easy thumb rules. Therefore, all 'new-age' ideas of mass Kundalini awakening are perfect nonsense because the energy of Kubjika is guhyati guhya.

Saraswati in the Light of Sri Aurobindo's Writings

Across India, especially in the north and eastern India, including Nepal, Vasant Panchami is the day when one of the cardinal goddesses of Hinduism, Devi Saraswati is worshipped. This falls on the fifth day in the month of Magha during the time of the spring. Some scholars believe that the linking of Goddess Saraswati with Vasanta Panchami comes from the later day Brahma Vaivarta Purana, where Sri Krishna orders the worship of Devi Saraswati on this particular Panchami *tithi*. Artists, writers, students and just about anyone involved in any kind of creative endeavour seeks benedictions of this form of the Divine Mother to enable them to excel in their chosen field of self-expression.

Saraswati is one of the earliest names of the goddess, and a redoubtable member of the Vedic pantheon that comes to us from the time of the *Rig Veda* itself. The eponymous River Saraswati is considered a central icon of the Vedic era, and even in the post-Vedic texts, it is referred to with tremendous reverence. We are told that the early Vedic people lived along the banks of this river, just as most ancient civilizations flourished on the banks of major rivers, and over time, elevated the physical river to the status of a life-giving goddess. While this naturalistic explanation certainly has some scriptural backing, including from the Mahabharata which mentions the drying up of the Saraswati River, there is also another way of looking at the whole Saraswati phenomenon. She is in Her true scope and manifestation, when seen in a purely Vedantic light, nothing less than a phenomenon par excellence, especially in contrast with the frailty and ignorance of the limited human consciousness.

Saraswati can mean 'she of the stream, the flowing movement', and is, therefore, a natural name for a river, but it also means eloquence and the power of speech, as also a movement of inspiration. In spiritual terms, any force or capacity, like speech, is a Shakti and a manifestation of the Divine Mother. Saraswati is also referred to as Mahi, meaning vast or great, and found, at times, mentioned in connection with two other names, Ila and Bharati.

इला सरस्वती महि तिस्रो देवीर्मयोभुवः
बर्हिः सीदन्त्वस्रिधः

Sri Aurobindo's commentary of this verse is as follows:

'May Ila, Saraswati, and Mahi, three goddesses who give birth to the bliss, take their place on the sacrificial seat, they who stumble not,' or 'who come not to hurt' or 'do no hurt'.

The epithet means, I think, they in whom there is no false movement with its evil consequences, duritam, no stumbling into pitfalls of sin and error. The formula is expanded in Hymn 110 of the tenth Mandala:

आ नो यज्ञं भारति तूयं एतु
इला मनुष्वद् इह चेतयन्ती

तिस्रो देवीर्बर्हिरेदम् स्योनम्
सरस्वती स्वपशः सदन्तु

(May Bharati come speeding to our sacrifice and Ila hither awakening our consciousness (or, knowledge or perceptions) in human wise, and Saraswati—three goddesses sit on this blissful seat, doing well the Work.)

Thus, Ila and Bharati are similar powers of the Divine Mother, similar to Saraswati yet with slight and nuanced differences. While Saraswati is the inspiration that comes down to us from *rtam*, the tremendous Truth consciousness, Bharati and Ila are also different forms of the same energy. In a *rik* by Madhuchchhandas, in which Bharati is identified with Mahi, this deity, translated literally, is 'full of cows for the sacrificer'. To a naturalistic interpreter this may seem like a straight link between an agrarian society's high regard for bovine wealth, but by this kind of logic, many verses of the Veda appear as meaningless ramblings of prehistoric barbarians. That does not do justice to the belief passed down since the ancient times that the Vedic verses were 'seen' by Rishis in a state of Divine inspiration containing lofty spiritual truths, which can be properly understood only by *tapasya* and sadhana, not mere scholastic or intellectual readings.

In one of Vamadeva's hymns in the fourth Mandala (IV.3.16), the rishi describes himself as one illumined, expressing through his thought and speech, words of guidance, 'secret words' —*ninya vachamsi*—'seer-wisdoms that utter their inner meaning to the seer'—*kavyani kavaye nivachana*. The rishi Dirghatamas speak of the *riks*, the Mantras of the Veda, as existing 'in a supreme ether, imperishable and immutable in which all the gods are seated', and he adds 'one who knows not That, what shall he do with the Rik?' (I.164.39). It becomes clear therefore that even when the Vedic Age was in full force, the verses of the Vedas acted as symbols of higher spiritual truths. 'Go', therefore, is both cow and light—a spiritual illumination so prized by our rishis. Thus, Bharati is the Shakti that is filled with a greater illumination which, when invoked, shares a portion of Her exalted status with the performer of the sacrifice.

While delving more into this we might as well recall a bit from Sri Aurobindo's own writings, about how he came across the Vedic corpus for the first time. Of course, some may or may not like his writings; regardless, it is vital that the following passage is quoted, lest some are led to ignorantly believe that the man was commenting without sufficient tapasya or sadhana.

My first contact with Vedic thought came indirectly while pursuing certain lines of self-development in the way of Indian yoga, which, without my knowing it, were spontaneously converging towards the ancient and now unfrequented paths followed by our forefathers. At this time there began to arise in my mind an arrangement of symbolic names attached to certain psychological experiences, which had begun to regularize themselves; and among them there came the figures of three female energies, Ila, Saraswati, Sarama, representing severally three out of the four faculties of the intuitive reason—revelation, inspiration and intuition.

- Sri Aurobindo, The Secret of the Veda

Much later when he was in Pondicherry and on an *adesha* from Krishna and started studying and meditating on the *Rig Veda*, did he recognize that the three goddesses he had seen earlier were Vedic deities.

Coming back to Saraswati and Her sister goddesses, we find Mahi is associated with, apart from illumination, a sense of vastness, *brihat*, which contains within Herself the Truth, Satyam. Ila, on the other hand, means She who attains and contains a similar association of ideas as rishi or *rtam*. Thus, Ila is the goddess who sees, or grants the ability of direct perception of spiritual planes and realities. While Saraswati represents the ability to hear the inspired word, and during normal functioning, is the goddess who provides inspiration for creativity. In other words, when the mind becomes more supple in deeper states of meditation and goes beyond the churning of the rationalizing machine, certain kinds of powers of intuition manifest themselves to the sadhaka. Of these, the access to an intuitive revelation—like a vision seen within which is true—is represented by the Goddess Ila; while Saraswati is one who brings about shruti or occult, inspired hearing, analogous to a voice that speaks within and provides inspired inputs.

These fine distinctions, however, came to be neglected later on as Saraswati became associated with 'learning'—a crude derivative of Her Vedic nature—while Bharati got merged into her and Ila just vanished, and a later story of another Ila came about in relation to the life of the graha Buddha! Moreover, as the age of Tantra and Puranas gained prominence, these triple goddesses became represented in the three rivers: Ganga, Yamuna and Saraswati, or the three channels inside the subtle body, namely, Ida, Pingla and Kundalini, where Saraswati became representative of the subtler Sushumna, equivalent to the vanished river of Vedic era.

Although we now associate Saraswati with learning or education, she is certainly not the goddess of fact accumulation, which passes as knowledge these days. She is rather the inspiration of the artist and the creator, of the architect and poet, of the scientist, of all who stand at the forefront of the masterful application of human knowledge and potential. Sri Aurobindo writes:

Mahasaraswati is the Mother's Power of Work and her spirit of perfection and order. The science and craft and technique of things are Mahasaraswati's province. Always she holds in her nature and can give to those whom she has chosen the intimate and precise knowledge, the subtlety and patience, the accuracy of intuitive mind and conscious hand and discerning eye of the perfect worker.

In the famous Devi Mahatyam, which comes from the *Markandeya Purana,* we find Mahasaraswati as the presiding deity of the third section of the text. In Shakti sadhana, there are three fundamental aspects: an awakening of Shakti, a holding of Shakti and the application of the same. Each of these is progressively more difficult. Thus, while many may awaken Shakti by dint of sadhana, only a few are then able to hold it in their mind and body, and even lesser learn how to apply the same. And this, the third part, is where the real guidance of Mahasaraswati becomes vital to the sadhaka.

Where reason cannot reach even by laboured meandering advances, intuition prompts us in the right direction. Of all forms of the Divine Mother, it is Mahasaraswati that demands of us infinite patience and a vast capacity for work. Because intuition of creativity does not come when sitting idle, it comes unannounced when we are completely absorbed in our work; the deeper the engagement the greater is the possibility of opening the consciousness to the play of Mahasaraswati, who nudges us slightly but persistently towards a greater and more accurate perfection of the work.

Bhairavi

One of the most important goddesses in the Mahavidya pantheon is Bhairavi, a term that has wide application and meaning in the tantric tradition. Sometimes she appears as the fifth and sometimes as the sixth in the list of Mahavidyas. Bhairavi, the goddess, is not to be confused with the eponymous raga of the Indian classical music though there may be some vague correlation between the time of the day connected to the raga and this Mahavidya.

Bhairavi means one who inspires terror or awe; she is oftentimes referred to with a more formal name—Tripura-Bhairavi—goddess of the three places, towns or *pura*, which some yogis identify with the three states of *jagrat* (waking), *swapna* (dreaming) and *sushupti* (sleeping). In another way of interpretation, it may also represent the three worlds of the material, subtle and causal, beyond which lie the fourth and powerful realm of authentic spirituality. Bhairavi, in the Mahavidya pantheon, is that terrifying force, which destroys all that blocks a Seeker or makes him persist in these three lower and more mundane states of reality, allowing an unhindered ascension to the condition of Turiya or true *adhaytma*. Destruction, of course, is fundamental to the path of Tantra, as can be seen from the eulogy offered to the Divine Mother in the Chandipath with the shloka:

सृष्टि स्थिति विनाशानां शक्तिभूते सनातने
कादिः काली महाशक्तिः हादिः त्रिपुरसुन्दरी
कादित्वाद् ब्रह्मरुपात्वम् हादित्वाद् शिवरुपता

Iconography

In the traditional Shakta tantric texts, Bhairavi is represented as a goddess with the splendour of a thousand suns. She has three eyes, wears a diadem of rare and precious gems, shaped to represent a crescent moon. Her face is as beautiful as a full-blown lotus flower, with kind eyes and a smiling disposition. She adorns a red dress, her breasts are blood-smeared, wearing a garland of human skulls, a rosary and book in one hand, and a *jnana mudra* and *varada mudra* in the other two. She sits on a lotus asana, sometimes on a corpse, radiating a beauty so stunning that all who see her Divine countenance are struck with awe and wonder. In another description of Tripura Bhairavi from the Kalika Purana, we find her with bows, arrows, rosary and a book, while standing in *samapada* on the back of a *preta*, who is carried by four other pretas. A variation of this iconography represents her standing or sitting on one preta, who is later identified as Sadashiva. She is thus described as sitting in a half-lotus posture on the heart of

Sadashiva, who is shown laughing. Around her neck is a garland of human heads, freshly cut with blood dripping, mixed with a garland of red flowers reaching up to her feet; she has uplifted breasts, four arms, naked, with a rosary in her upper right arm, boon granting mudra in her lower right arm, *abhaya mudra* in her upper left and a book in her lower left arm. Three eyes, a smiling face and a love for streaming blood is also mentioned in the text in connection to Bhairavi.

In the later tantric texts like *Bhairavayamala* and the eventual authoritative compendium called *Tantrasara* (sixteenth century), Bhairavi spawns derivative goddesses like the ten-armed Rudra Bhairavi, who is Shivasimhasanasthitam—residing on a throne made of Shiva's body. By this time, we find a universal modification of the iconographic seat of Bhairavi from lotus to corpse whose identity oscillates between Shiva and Mahapreta. Texts such as *Shakta Pramoda* describe her as being fond of meat, alcohol and cremation grounds, where she hunts for consuming the flesh of all who once had prana flowing in their system, making them animated, but have now died.

One possible reason as to why the seat of Tripura Bhairavi underwent a change from the lotus to a Mahapreta could be that the practices related to Bhairavi, especially in the sampradayas of eastern India, became associated with the left-hand path, or *vamachara*, that necessarily involves ritual setting of a cremation ground and other heterodox paraphernalia.

In the esoteric parlance, Bhairavi is the goddess of constant destruction, unlike say Chinnamasta, whose effect is stunning and sudden destruction, when needed. Every process that leads one to death, physical or emotional, is by the power of Bhairavi. So, yogis considered all movement of the *apana vayu*, in fact anything that leads to death and decay, which governs natural bodily functions like defecation, urination, loss of sexual fluids, aging, and eventually death are all under the exclusive power of Bhairavi.

She is also supposed to exist in the *mooladhara* chakra from where she starts her play as the awakened Kundalini, thus destroying and transcending (both are essentially the same) each of the lower *tattvas* one at a time. In this sense, in the inner yYoga, which is so often referred to in tantric texts and passed down traditionally from Guru to *shishya*, Tripura Bhairavi's power can help a *sadhaka* in going beyond and understanding the essential nature and application of the *prithivi, jala* and agni tattva in the body and all around in the world. In fact, She is also known as the *tapas*, or inner spiritual heat generated by the force of *sadhana*. While it is the nature and peculiar power of an awakened Kundalini to be able to self-identify with anything, from a deity to a speck of dust, whatever the sadhaka chooses to self-identify with, no other form of Mahavidya is so strongly equated to the force of an awakened Kundalini as Tripura Bhairavi is. In other words, Bhairavi is the personification of Kundalini's terrific power of destroying and altering all the old perceptions, mechanical thinking, customary habits, and unexamined routine ideas, which can and must happen, before this all-powerful Shakti can go into subtler realms and higher chakras and change a *pashu* into a *nara*. And this power of endless destruction is why the goddess is known as Bhairavi, meaning 'terrifying'.

Advaita scholars interpreting the Mahavidya have considered Tripura Bhairavi to be equivalent to *paravak*, or the primordial unmanifest speech. However, this may not be consistent with the ideas about Bhairavi expressed in Tantras, or with the experience of those who have performed *upasana* of this form. It is rather likely that this equivalence was drawn up using a pseudo-similarity between *para*, which by some accounts starts from mooladhara, and the association of Bhairavi with the said chakra. This author is of the firm opinion that true *paravak* is a function of the *mahakarana*, greater causal body, and as such, practically, inaccessible to 99 per cent of the sadhakas.

Technically, however, Tripura Bhairavi is closely related to the other Mahavidya goddess with the Tripura epithet, namely Tripurasundarii or sodasi. This falls under the *hadi krama*, more popularly known as Srikula. A verse from the *Mahakala Samhiti* settles the matter of distribution between vidyas.

कादिः काली महाशक्तिः हादिस्त्रिपुरसुन्दरी ।
कादित्वाद् ब्रह्मरूपत्वं हादित्वाच्छिवरूपता ॥

It is generally accepted that while the Kalikula relates to the *kadikrama*, and the Srikula uses the hadikrama, while Mahavidya Tara, according to some traditions, forms a link between the kadi and hadi vidyas.

Owing to Bhairavi's irresistible power of causing decay and destruction, many early writers have used terms like Ghora, Kalaratri and *mahapralaya* to describe her devastating power.

Sadhana

The *upasana* of Tripura Bhairavi is entirely tantric and must be undertaken only under the guidance of a Guru who is well versed in this, and who belongs to a *parampara* where this form of Mahashakti has been worshipped. Tripura Bhairavi has many different forms as well. The *Tantrasara* describes 12 such forms: Sampatprada Bhairavi, Sakalasiddhi Bhairavi, Bhayavinashini Bhairavi, Chaitanya Bhairavi, Bhuvaneshwari Bhairavi, Kameshwari Bhairavi, Annapurneshwari Bhairavi, Nitya Bhairavi, Rudra Bhairavi, Bhadra Bhairavi, Subhamkari Bhairavi and Smashana Bhairavi. Each of them has their specialized domains, as evident from the names. While Chaitanya Bhairavi awakens the divine consciousness, Kameshwari Bhairavi grants desires and Annapurneshwari provides sustenance.

In the Mahavidya tradition, Tripura Bhairavi's consort is Kalabhairava and her upasana is said to remove all obstructions and break down every shackle that can tie an individual—physically or psychologically. Further, in *jyotisha*, Bhairavi is invoked for *lagna shuddhi,* or protecting the native in case the *lagna* is afflicted severely. References to this goddess can be found even in the Devi Mahatyam along with a description of her forms. In some *sampradayas*, it is believed that the specific form of the Mahashakti who consumes alcohol before destroying Mahishasura was none other than Tripura Bhairavi. Another story related to the Mahavidya tradition mentions that Tripura Bhairavi is the only form of Shakti which speaks to Shiva directly.

From this goddess, we have a more ubiquitous use of the term Bhairavi in the eastern and northern tantric sampradayas where Bhairavi is an accomplished woman *sadhika*, who has been given appropriate *diksha* and who is well versed in Shakti sadhana. Oftentimes, expert Bhairavis have acted as gurus to neophyte sadhakas. In colloquial knowledge, a Bhairavi is also known to freely use her sexual energies for the purpose of sadhana and remains unconstrained by societal dos and don'ts. At the same time, this is not a licence for promiscuous behaviour. In fact, without a Bhairavi diksha, no one can enter this path, leave alone achieve any true benefits of Shakti sadhana. Among Bhairavis too there is a further classification known as Mahabhairavis, whose process of diksha and methods of sadhana are kept hidden from the public. The krama of a Bhairavi sadhana starts with an expertise in the methods of yoni puja. Yoni is considered in Tantra as symbolic of the Divine womb from which creation occurs. As such everything in practical tantric worship is designed by keeping in mind not only the rituals but also the symbolism of various worldly things and their relation to the spiritual or supernatural realm. Thus, during the ritual, women are to be looked at as the insignia of

Shakti, while men become the insignia of *adhara*—the vehicle that carries, or rather moderates and shapes a particular Shakti. Shiva is therefore considered the greatest of all adhara. There is, however, one form of Shakti which is considered *niradhara*, which needs no support, which is almost transcendental, and who is, in this theology, the originator of everything, from gods to asuras to men to animals, plants and insects.

The second schematic aspect of any tantric upasana is related to the five *tattvas—prithvi, apas*, agni, vayu and akasha. It is in purifying these tattvas that take up a major chunk of the practice and then reading them accurately at any given time and performing ritual actions that are supposed to give best results in a particular combination prevalent among the tattvas. In that sense, it is believed that certain kinds of women can take to Bhairavi upasana better than others, as the tattvas in their mind-body are better aligned. Ganika, Nati, Chandali are mentioned in texts as women who have the five pranas and five tattvas perfectly aligned in their mind-body, who when initiated into the path, can become excellent Bhairavis.

A large part of the Bhairavi sadhana includes a *nyasa*-like ritual, kept hidden from the merely curious, where different mantras and devatas are invoked onto every limb of the Bhairavi. This, when perfected, makes the sadhikas very presence Divine and spiritually potent. The male consort of such a Bhairavi is referred to as Bhairava, reminiscent of the unorthodox form of Shiva, who is known to break all boundaries. The Bhairavi sadhanas used to be performed in a circle of initiated sadhakas, known as the Bhairavi Chakra, where each Bhairava, a male initiate, would sit such that his partner or Bhairavi would be sitting towards the left, while the proceedings of the ritual would be conducted under the joint guidance of the *chakreshwar* and his consort known as *chakreshwari*. The influence of chakra and Bhairavi sadhana spread quickly across medieval India, such that cults of various other devatas too incorporated newer tantric iconographies in their midst that have a direct link to these practices. For example, in the form of Ucchista Ganpati we find a nude consort sitting on the left lap of Ganesha, and the ithyphallic devata caressing the genitalia of the naked goddess. This form is very typically reminiscent of the Bhairavi sadhanas of Tantra marg, for this posture is replicated by the Bhairava and Bhairavi while performing practices involving sexual intercourse, of a sublimated and ritualized variety. Again, this should not be viewed from the confused blinkers of Abrahamic morality, for these Bhairavi sadhanas were anything but normal carnal indulgence. After the puja is completed, the Bhairava and the Bhairavi would then perform the *shovini mudra* while unifying themselves and at the same time keeping their concentration fixed on the heart or the Agya, as needed for their mutual development. A telltale sign of authentic Bhairavis would be their ability to look physically much younger than their chronological age, a power that comes from the Goddess Bhairavi's exceptional governance of and control over all aging processes.

These days, of course, such practices have almost vanished, except maybe when performed in secrecy in places like Kamakhya.

There is no single famous temple dedicated to this form. However, there are many temples of Patala Bhairavi in different cities like Ujjain, Bhopal, certain towns in Odisha, etc. There is also a Siddha Bhairavi temple in Ganjam, Brahmapur. A cave dedicated to Goddess Bhairavi in the Nilachal Parvat of Kamrupa is an active place of Bhairavi worship, with a long-standing tradition of *chakra puja* extending from the time when a Bhairavi Siddha tantric used to live there at least a century ago.

Thus, Tripura Bhairavi in the Mahavidya tradition is easily the closest representation of the Kundalini's first outburst—that aspect of the universal Mahashakti Jagadamba, which has transcended the ordinary material life and opened up other invisible occult worlds and experiences, and in doing so destroyed and regenerated, when allowed to play in her full capacity, all the old psychological mores of the practitioner. Nothing destroys as powerfully and completely everything in the lower triple world—*bhur, bhuvah, svah*—which we inhabit as the grace of Bhairavi does. And in so doing, She saves us from ourselves and leads the sadhaka on the road to a greater peace and fulfillment.

Chinnamasta

⋯⋯⋆⋯⋯

Among the various Mahavidyas, arguably the most awe-inspiring iconography is that of Goddess Chinnamasta. Depending on the progression followed, she appears fifth or sixth in the list of Mahavidyas. Not just in Hindu Tantra, Chinnamasta finds herself ensconced in the pantheon of Tibetan tantric deities as Vajravairochani. Her stunningly ferocious imagery naturally invokes fear and trepidation, matched only by the effects that her *sadhana* can cause to a Seeker.

In Tibetan Buddhism theogony, she is also referred to as Chinnamunda, who, some scholars believe is a form of Vajravarahi. The term '*vajra*' denotes an indestructible purity and is often added as a prefix to the names of different spiritual beings. One of the earliest texts which mention Chinnamasta is the Hindu *Chinnamastakalpa* and the *Tantrasara*. The latter is the most authentic sadhana compendium for almost all Kalikula practices and it is among this particular stream of Shaktas where *upasana* of Chinnamasta has been popular historically. The Buddhist equivalent text is the *Sadhanamala* of the twelfth century, where details of Vajravairochani mantra, Tantra, and sadhana have been mentioned. Whatever be her exact origins, by the ninth century she was already an established Mahavidya among the tantrics.

Iconography

The typical iconography of the goddess depicts her in a deep red colour of a hibiscus flower, radiating the effulgence of a million suns. Digambari, with a *munda-mala* (skull garland) and a snake for her *yagyopavita*, standing in the *pratyalidha* posture, she has cut off her own head and holds it in one of her hands. From her neck erupts three streams of blood, which is eagerly consumed by her attendants on two sides, *dakini* and *varini*. The third stream goes into her own severed head, which she holds in her left hand. Her other hand holds a *khadga*, and oftentimes she has a blue lotus in her heart.

Various scholars have tried to decode and read different meanings into this awe-inspiring imagery, including some like the very learned Shankaranarayan, who finds Vedic imports in the origin and symbolism of Chinnamasta. He writes:

(she) is the thunderclap and the lightning flash, shining like a streak of lightning (vidyullekheva bhasvara). That is why Chinnamasta is known as Vajravairochaniya. She is the force of Virochana, the especially luminous (visesena rocate'iti virochanah). Who is Virochana? The Supreme itself, the primodial prakasha. Vajra is her power which

he wields. We know Vajra is the weapon of Indra... in the Veda, the paramount deity.

However, the imagery lends itself to a less strenuous and more comprehensive explanation using standard tantric concepts. The three bloodstreams symbolized the three fundamental ethereal nerves inside the subtle body—Ida, Pingla and Sushumna. Blood is generally considered to be the best representative of prana inside a human being. Hence, the *vamachari* preference for blood-drinking goddesses—symbolizing *raktashuddhi* and the more practical manifestation of blood sacrifices.

The heart of tantric sadhana and prayogas lie in the use of exact ingredients at the right time for the perfect ritual. Nothing is arbitrary or whimsically done. Prana, which keeps us alive and ties the mind to the body while we live, can be used along with the *apanavayu* to awaken inside the human mind-body complex that misunderstood yet inexplicably powerful spiritual power named Kundalini. While Ida and Pingla are important for balancing and controlling our daily psychology, Kundalini passing through the Sushumna comes into play when the first contact with an otherworldly spiritual atmosphere is made such that our sense of reality starts changing, hopefully for the better. But what about the severed head? The journey of the Kundalini is meant to continue until it reaches the top of the head and merges into the Sahasrar. This is another way of saying that the Kundalini can go up to the final destination only when the constant churning of the normal mind is forced to stop. Nobody whose mind runs around like a monkey on a roller coaster can ever seriously hope to experience the full awakening of the Kundalini Shakti. Thus, Chinnamasta is the form of Adya Kali, who cuts off the rationalizing mind in one shot and pushes the tremendous force of Kundalini right onto the top of the skull with the speed of a lightning strike! Given the abruptness and exceptional danger involved in this process, very few people really have the nerves needed to experience or perform a successful sadhana of this form. No wonder the *Tantrasara* calls her Prachanda Chandika (Chandi herself being fierce, Prachanda Chandika is super fierce) as well as Sarvasiddhi, who grants all *siddhis*. The Sadhanamala describes her as *sarvabuddhi*— complete intelligence, or enlightened intelligence. This author has seen even tantric adepts with decades of experience overcome by fear when attempting to perform Chinnamasta upasana. Naturally, such sadhana requires an appropriate setting which adheres to the recommendations of Tantra sadhana and a competent Guru who can judge if a sadhaka is capable of this practice. Another vital element in the iconography is the fact that Chinnamasta stands on two copulating bodies. Celibacy is of great importance, at least during the initial phases, for the practice to succeed and cause no harm to the practitioner.

Antiquity

Chinnamasta is also known as Vajravairochani. Vairochana is related to sun or fire, to be of a solar disposition. Vajra is not just a thunderbolt but also something adamantine or impenetrable. Vajravairochani is the force of an adamantine, inexhaustible fire. This etymology has led many sadhakas and scholars to speculate that this Mahavidya is best experienced when the Kundalini, which is often equated with subtle fire, awakens with a deadly force from the Manipura Chakra at the solar plexus of the body. The most commonly used mantra of Chinnamasta refers to the goddess as Vajravairochani.

However, another simpler explanation for the suffix *vajra* is the link that the deity bears to the Vajrayana tradition of Tibet. It has left scholars speculating whether Chinnamasta was originally a Hindu deity or a Buddhist goddess imported into Hinduism. The texts which contain the dhyana references to the goddess are later compositions and as such not of much help with determining the accurate time of these. In the Buddhist compendium *Sadhanamala*, we find Vajrayogini, an *anuttarayoga ishta devata*, bears a surprising iconographic similarity with Chinnamasta. Vajrayogini is considered to be a deity with supreme control over the intermediate states between death and rebirth and have over centuries gathered a standalone cult of practitioners who approach her both for mundane and the supernal realizations. The most common epithet used to describe Vajrayogini and one that is used in the mantras given in *Sadhanamala* is Sarvabuddhadakini, a *dakini* who is the essence of all Buddhas, while her companions, as per this compendium, are Vajravarnini and Vajravairochani. Scholars are of the opinion that the *Sadhanamala*, which contains about 300 different practices, was composed somewhere around the fifth century AD, and therefore it would not be unreasonable to assume that Chinnamasta or Vajrayogini had already developed into a mature practice by the time this text was written down.

A crucial part of any tantric sadhana is application or prayoga, which is different from mukti. Philosophically there is no conflict in keeping a greater focus on application or using the power of a deity only for the limited purpose of a specific prayoga, instead of performing the sadhana for a great spiritual benefit. Chinnamasta sadhanas, given the extremely ferocious nature of the deity, are most often used to bring about the destruction of one's enemies. Sadhakas have recorded the effects that this deity has on the mind, creating a great sense of fear in some cases, and then teaching the practitioner to overcome that fear. The sadhana also involves sexual continence, for she stands on Kamadeva and Rati, and the power generated through the control of sexual energy is then used to push the Kundalini Shakti into the central channel of the subtle body known as the Sushumna. However, the Buddhist tradition worship of Yabyum deities, of which Vajrayogini can be an element, does require a suitable partner if the fifth *makara* is to be performed. Unknown to casual readers, the original mantra sadhana of Chinnamasta involved an invocation not only to Chinnamasta but also to her companions dakini and *varini*. Here too we find the *Sadhanamala* using triple *beejas*, probably to represent each of the three deities in the full pantheon. This format, of course, underwent many changes with the *Tantrasara*, among other texts, prescribing many variations of the beejas used in the Chinnamasta *moolmantra*. Apart from texts, of course, there is also a vast living tradition and wealth of information on the goddess, and the effects of the sadhana as passed down in various Kaula *paramparas*. For example, when Chinnamatsa *homas* are performed using *Combretum indicium*, one may attain *vaksiddhi*; while using Plumeria flowers may grant a sadhaka great sukh. Similarly, white *Thevetia peruviana* used in Chinnamasta fire ritual frees one from all kinds of diseases, the red version of the same flower generates *akarshan* shakti in the sadhaka. Some even use dhatura—a species of poisonous vespertine flowering plants—for some of the more dangerous prayogas using Chinnamasta mantras.

A less ambitious application of Chinnamasta sadhana is for nullifying the effects of Rahu as a *graha*. Probably the most important centre of Chinnamasta worship in India exists in Rajarappa in the state of Jharkhand. Located at the confluence of the Bhairavi *nadi* and the Damodar *nad* (male river), it has been a place of great reverence for people of the state as well as devotees from Bihar and West Bengal. After a theft and desecration in the temple in 2010, artisans from Rajasthan were called to remake the idol carved out of dark Hessonite, or *gomedh*, which is the recommended stone for Rahu, and thereafter a nine-day *pranapratishtha* ritual and Chinnamasta homa were conducted.

But Kamya prayogas are not the only way to approach this deity. They may be popular no doubt, but history is not without great sadhakas who have approached her for communion and spiritual uplift. An oft-repeated caveat must be in place. All such practices need the guidance of a Guru who knows the path. These are too dangerous for casual experimentation and may complicate matters in the hands of novices. Raja Krishnachandra of Bengal, a contemporary of the Shakta-poet Ramprasad Sen, was reputed to be a sadhaka of Chinnamasta. The tantric author Taranath mentions that Kanipa or Krishacharya, one of the 84 Mahasiddhas of Tibetan Buddhism, had two female disciples from Maharashtra, namely Mekhala and Kanakhala, who were experts in Chinnamasta sadhana, having attained communion with the goddess. These two female adepts were also considered Mahasiddhas in the tradition. In the Hindu Mahavidya tradition, Chinnamasta is accompanied by Krodha Bhairava, and among the 24 avatars of Vishnu mentioned in the *Bhagwatam*, Chinnamasta is equivalent to the Narasimha avatar.

Finally, the most beautiful aspect (for awe and beauty can go hand in hand) of her unique imagery is the fact that it is her own decapitated head that drinks the blood gushing out of her neck. No better symbolism could have captured the Vedantic truth of the all-pervading Brahma, who is both everything and nothing— Herself the sacrifice, Herself the sacrificer, Herself the sacrificed.

Garuda

꙳

Garuda is the mythical bird in Hinduism, who acts as the vehicle of Lord Vishnu. In the Adi Parva of the great epic of Vyasa, retold by Vaisampayana at the *sarpasatra* of King Janmejaya, and further narrated by Ugrasrava Sauti to the host of rishis headed by Saunaka, we find the story of this invincible Garuda.

Once Rishi Kashyapa was performing a fire sacrifice (yajna) for a desirable offspring. He had asked all devatas to assist him in the same. The mighty Indra, king of the devas, was assigned the task of bringing fuel for this grand sacrifice. As he flew through the sky carrying a heavy piece of wood, he looked down and saw a vast multitude of the Valakhilya rishis—by some accounts sixty thousand in number—struggling to carry a single stalk of the Palash leaf. Apart from being thumb-sized, the severity of their ascetic practices had resulted in their physical body becoming emaciated and weak, which made the task of carrying a single leaf appear extremely difficult. A watery depression along their path caused by the hoof of a cow posed an insurmountable obstacle for these miniature rishis. Drunk as he was with the arrogance of his own might, Indra stopped and laughed at their misery, insulted them thus and finally flew over their head without offering any assistance. This angered the Valakhilyas and filled them with a terrible resolve. They decided to create another being, more powerful than Indra, who would move at the speed of thought, who could muster any amount of strength as the occasion demanded, who would be unbeatable in war and unmatched in ferocity, who could strike fear in the heart of Indra and finally be the one to replace the Lord of the devas. With this intention in mind, they participated in the yajna of Kashyapa, pronouncing powerful mantras to aid their cause.

Indra was terrified when he realized what had happened and what was about to happen. He rushed to Rishi Kashyapa, explaining everything and begging to be rescued. Kashyapa then went to the Valakhilyas and asked them if they were satisfied with the sacrifice. Tied to a vow of truth-speaking, the Valakhilyas disclosed to Kashyapa that they had set in motion a process by which a new Indra would be born. The mind-born son of Brahma then explained that Indra had been pronounced sovereign of the three worlds by the promise of Brahma. Trying to replace Indra would tantamount to falsifying the words of Brahma, which would be futile. To rescue the situation, Kashyapa suggested to let there be a new Indra, not of humans but of birds and winged creatures! The Valakhilyas, already pacified by now, agreed readily. This was how the mighty and fearless Garuda was born as the son of Rishi Kashyapa from his wife Vanita.

The Pouranik story of Garuda can be interpreted as a psychological description of certain spiritual states of a Seeker. If we look at the devas as various life-fulfilling and positive qualities in a man, and asuras and rakshasas represent all that is negative or animalistic in man, then Indra is the intellect, which lords over the various sensory inputs transmitted through the agency of the sense organs (*indriyas*). During the ancient times, Indra as a deity held a position of prestige and honour as evident from the various Vedic hymns attributed to him. However, by the time when Dwapara Yuga was to end and Kali Yuga was to begin, Indra lost his grandeur. Krishna, as the Srimad Bhagwatam mentions, forbade residents of Vrindavana from worshipping Indra. When the human intellect is subtle, it can directly perceive spiritual truths and subliminal realities. But as the quality of time progressively deteriorates from Satya Yuga to the Kali Yuga, the nature of the average intellect too degrades, making a direct intellectual realization of a higher and deeper reality, far more difficult if not impossible. When a certain rigidity of the mind and thought gets added to this spiritual impotency of the intellect, it compounds the problem manifold, resulting in a mental fanaticism that is often a precursor to practical fanaticism, exhibiting itself through a mindless affinity for dogmas, religious or otherwise, that have outlived their purpose. The next obvious step to this mental fanaticism is arrogance and supremacist behaviour. This is the essential reason why Krishna stops the worship of Indra and tells him while diffusing Indra's delusions of grandeur in the Govardhan episode, that he (Indra), unlike in an earlier era, has become arrogant and overconfident. Consequently, we hardly find any temple dedicated entirely to Indra. But if Indra is the normal human intellect, what then is Garuda?

The average human mind functions through a rigorous and fragmented labour of reason and piecemeal logic. It is however eminently possible, employing serious effort and practice to push beyond the abilities of the normal mind and experience a larger integrative quality of thought. As the mind expands, so does its basic nature and operating principle. It acquires an equanimous ability to handle apparently contradictory information in the right balance and flow with abundant ease, and without being swept, stressed or disturbed, residing in a greater stillness and calm. Even further as it goes, a definitive and unfailing intuition starts pouring in and directing the Seeker. This is what the imagery of Hari riding the Garuda represents. Garuda is the Indra—the vast and powerful lord for all that flies above the normal human mind—practically manifesting in a Seeker as the activation of a greater, more supple and more subtle intellect, while Vishnu is the spotless Divine intuition that rides this new and fitter vehicle. Garuda moves at the speed of thought because it is a higher and superior kind of thought itself; it is fearless because an exalted mind which can see things from multiple sides has no cause for fear; it is unassailable (by human negatives) because it abides in detachment and objectivity; it is wise because true wisdom is a natural byproduct of such a mental condition, and it is unfailing because it is ever guided by the Supreme all-seeing intelligence. And it is this spiritual state, as it becomes a settled realization, that can bring the nectar of causeless *ananda* (amrita) to the Seeker.

Garuda is the greatest enemy of the Nagas. The Adi Parva of the Mahabharata states that the Nagas, born of Kadru and fathered by the same Rishi Kashyapa, were a bickering lot, steeped in jealousy, rancour and possessiveness. To make the normal human mind ascend to the status of a Garuda, it is imperative that the

Seeker must move beyond all that constricts the consciousness. Steady detachment is the perfect antithesis to low pettiness. Unlike the others, the Shesha Naga, who remained unaffected by the environment of low intrigue that surrounded him and eventually disassociated himself from the other Nagas, was bestowed with the title of Ananta (Infinity) by the creator. He too finds a place in the pantheon of Vishnu and becomes a friend of the mighty Garuda. It is interesting that both Garuda and the Nagas, though diametrically opposite by nature, are fathered by the same individual. A human being may choose to plunge into lowly depth or ascend to masterly heights.

When we look at the above from the perspective of Kundalini yoga, we can explain this phenomenon as the rise of Shakti above the head. This automatically causes a terrific, impregnable silence to descend on the mind, accompanied by a commanding Divine guidance, which cannot be disobeyed.

A mind that tears itself away from the tyranny of ceaseless and unwashed thoughts, operating from a much higher station of equanimity, selflessness and accompanying wisdom and compassion is the spiritual essence of the iconography showing the Supreme (Hari) astride the transformed mind (Garuda).

Forms and Non-Duality

❦

Many non-dualists of today believe that 'deities are just projections of the ego', implying that it is futile to run after them. This stems from a misreading of non-duality, both in theory and practice. Every individual has an I-sense, the ego. Is the whole world a projection of the individual's I-sense? Not really. One's own ego creates the immediate environment but has no effect or influence on the existence or non-existence of far-off objective realities. Which means the President of the United States is not a projection of someone's ego, neither are the Himalayas. But our life circumstances, friends, family, relatives, office, our joys, and sorrows are certainly projections of and entanglements of our ego. When the path of inquiry is followed to the logical end, the complete and total conclusion, then the individual I-sense dissolves and is replaced by a Universal I—literally the 'I' of the universe. Yes, for that magnificent 'I', every deity, every animate and inanimate being is but a projection of its own power and being. There is nothing anywhere that is not created by that great 'I'. The very same idea was beautifully conveyed by the Mother when someone asked her about creation and she replied, 'Where is the "I" in you that it can create anything substantial?' She was talking about that Universal I.

The full experience of the Self is very, very rare. Glimpses of it are common, especially if there is some *purva samskara*. Ramana Maharishi himself would differentiate between *manolaya* and *manonasha*—subduing of the mind temporarily to get a glimpse of the Self, and a complete destruction of the mind. The latter is the state to aim for and it is extremely difficult. It needs Grace and a physical Guru. When that happens, one encounters the Universal non-duality and everything becomes a projection of the Self with no independent existence. *Yatha pinde tatha brahmande* then becomes an actual reality for such a being. Before that supreme state is reached, mere glimpses of the Self is functionally analogous to closing your eyes in deep sleep, where the world may have vanished but the objective world is still perfectly in existence and it has an existence independent of the ego of a limited individual.

Now, what did Ramana think of forms? Ramana narrated that a *jnani* was once visited by deities and Siddhas. If everything is a projection of an individual's ego and the ego sense is obliterated in the Self, as it happened to Ramana, then how does he see deities or Siddhas? There can be only two explanations for this. One, as the Self takes control of the organism, one attains the *sakshi bhava*, sees everything but only like a distant old photograph with no attachment. The ego, whose job is to attach itself, no longer clings to the world of appearance or any so-called objective reality which enters its consciousness. But this theory can't explain the condition where everything is a projection of the Self. That is possible only when the individual I-sense has been destroyed and replaced by a universal I-sense, for lack of better words, the Self. To borrow a phrase from the great Srivaishnava metaphysical genius and spiritual master, Sri Ramanujacharya, the equation of God with the universe is like that of *sarira-sariri bhava*—the Supreme enters the Universe and governs it from within the way a body is governed by the soul. The universe is like an organism in which there is a grand I-sense exactly like humans have one, only this I-sense is the Universal or Cosmic Self, the God or Divine. Touch it once, and then everything from the oceans to the Himalayas will feel as a projection of oneself. However, this grand I is not the normal human ego at all. Reaching there and staying in that condition permanently is equivalent to the perfection of the Self experience and is extremely rare.

Ramana, as David Godman says in his research, changed his explanations with time to make it easier for people. This is because his earliest words were spoken from the standpoint of the perfected Self, while his later conversations were from a standpoint that would be easier for devotees to grasp, those who have not yet merged into the Self completely. Ramana makes this interesting statement that as long as the ego, or normal mind is working even to some degree, forms cannot be dropped. It is a practical impossibility. Hence, the need for Arunachala, or any other Divine name or form that the Seeker feels attracted to, or the need even for a Guru like Ramana, which is again a name and form. If one has perfectly obliterated the I-sense, such a mind needs no support. If not, then it will find whatever form or name it can and stick to it for existence.

To keep the mind preoccupied too much with philosophy can also be detrimental to spiritual growth. First experience the Self and then see which theory suits best. So how does a non-dualist reconcile devotion to any name or form? Divine names and forms are much beyond theories and explanations. All theories and explanations are man-made, they arise later, but formidable spiritual powerhouses like the holy mountain of Arunachala stands beyond time as it always has and always will. May it bestow the perfection of non-duality to all sincere seekers, and may it also protect from the errors of verbal and theoretical non-duality.

Om Shanti Shanti Shanti!

Glossary

Abhaya Mudra: *gesture indicating fearlessness*

Acamana: *purification ritual*

Acara: *mode of worship*

Acharya: *teacher of a spiritual subject*

Adesha: *a divine command*

Adhara: *mind-body complex*

Adharashuddhi: *purification of adhara of mind-body of sadhaka*

Adhidaivika Jagat: *world of gods*

Adhikara: *competency*

Adhyatma: *spirituality*

Adhyatmika Jagat: *world of atma*

Adi Parva: *first chapter*

Advaita Vedanta: *non-dual Vedanta*

Advaita: *non-dual*

Advaitic: *belonging to Advaita Vedanta*

Adya Kali: *the primal form of Kali*

Agama: *a kind of shastras*

Aghora: *a face of Shiva, also a sect of Saivas*

Agni: *fire*

Agya: *a chakra between the eyebrows*

Aham: *I-sense*

Aham Brahmansmi: *I am Brahman, (a statement in the Upanishads)*

Ahamkara: *ego*

Akarshan Shakti: *attraction power*

Akasha: *ether*

Akshobhya: *unshakeable, (a form of Shiva)*

Akula: *beyond the Kula, another name of Shiva*

Amarakosa: *a thesaurus in Sanskrit*

Amavasya: *dark phase of moon*

Amsha: *part*

Ananda: *bliss*

Ananta: *infinite*

Anga: *limb*

Ankusha: *goad to control elephants*

Annamaya-Kosha: *physical sheath*

Anugraha: *grace*

Apana Vayu: *lower moving vayu*

Apara Prakriti: *materialistic nature*

Aptavakta: *words of experts*

Artha: *wealth*

Aryaman: *Vedic God*

Asampradayavid: *without a sampradaya*

Asana: *seat*

Ashram: *hermitage*

Ashtami: *eighth tithi*

Ashva: *horse*

Asta Matrika: *eight matrikas worshipped*

Asura, Asuric: *negative malefic entities*

Atharvaveda: *the fourth Veda*

Atharvavedasakhini: *belonging to Atharva Veda*

Atimarga: *extreme path*

Atma: *eternal soul inside every being.*

Attahasa: *loud laughter*

Avidya: *ignorance*

Ayurveda: *traditional Hindu medical system*

Beeja: *seed*

Bhaga: *Vedic god*

Bhagwan: *god*

Bhairava: *Hindu deity*

Bhairavayamala: *a tantric text*

Bhairavi Chakra: *a circle of worship in tantra involving bhairavis*

Bhairavi: *form of goddess*

Bhasyas: *commentary*

Bhavatarini: *a form of Kali*

Bheda: *difference*

Bhikshatana Murti: *form of Shiva as a beggar*

Bhimarupi Maharudra: *a hymn to Hanuman*

Bhur: *physical plane*

Bhuta Yajna: *sacrificial ritual for bhutas*

Bhuta: *spirits of dead*

Bhutagni: *fire of intellectual digestion*

Bhuvah: *vital realm*

Brahma Vaivarta Purana: *a scripture*

Brahma: *creator deity of Hinduism*

Brahmahatya: *killing of Brahmin*

Brahman: *supreme reality*

Brahmanda Khappar: *skull of the universe*

Brihat: *vast*

Buddha: *founder of Buddhism*

Buddhi: *intelligence*

Buddhirupa: *form of intelligence*

Buddhishwari: *controller of intelligence*

Chaitya Purusha: *secret spiritual being in the heart*

Chakra Puja: *a form of puja where participants sit in a circle or chakra*

Chandabhairava: *a form of Bhairava*

Chandali: *a form of goddess very passionate and fierce*

Chandipath: *formal recitation of the Devi Mahatmam as a sadhana*

Charama Shloka: *ultimate sloka*

Chaturdasi tithi: *a tithi of the moon*

Chhanda: *meter of recitation*

Chinnamasta: *a Mahavidya devi*

Chit Shakti: *innate spiritual power*

Chitta: *the lower mind*

Cincini: *tamarind*

Dakini: *a female spiritual being*

Daksha Yajna: *yajna done by Daksha*

Dakshinamurti: *a form of Shiva, a Guru in meditation facing south*

Dasabhava: *attitude of a servant*

Desh-kaal-patra: *right time and context*

Deva Yajna: *ritual for gods*

Deva: *god*

Devata: *gods and deities*

Devi Mahatyam: *hymn to the goddess containing details of her battle against asuras*

Dhatura: *a poisonous plant*

Dhuni: *constantly burning fire maintained by some sect of sanyasis*

Digambari: *without clothes, sky clad*

Diksha: *initiation*

Divya: *divine*

Durga: *Hindu goddess*

Dvaita: *duality; a school of Vedanta*

Dwapara: *third of the four yugas defined in Hinduism*

Ekalinga: *single linga*
Ekjata: *form of Tara*

Gana: *one of the beings surrounding Shiva or Shakti*
Ganapataya: *follower of the sect of Ganpati*
Gandharva: *an ethereal being known for singing*
Ganga: *the river deemed sacred to Hindus*
Ganika: *refers to a prostitute*
Ganpati Atharvashira: *a hymn to Ganpati*
Garuda: *the great divine bird on whom Vishnu travels*
Ghora: *terrible*
Graha Budha: *the planet mercury*
Graha: *bodies that grasp consciousness used in jyotisha analysis*
Guhya Kali: *a rare form of Kali, secret Kali*
Guhyati Guhya: *secret of secrets*
Guna: *quality or attribute*
Guru: *spiritual master*
Gurumukhi: *from the Guru's mouth*
Gyanshakti: *power of wisdom*

Halahala: *poison*
Hanuman: *Hindu God who helped Rama in his epic battle against Ravana*
Hasti mukha: *elephant-faced*
Homa: *fire ritual*
Hridaya Guha: *cave of the heart*

Ichchashakti: *willpower*
Ida: *subtle channels inside human body*

Ila: *a form of Saraswati*

Indra: *Vedic deity*

Indriyas: *sense organs*

Ishta Devata: *worshipped deity*

Jagaran: *awakened*

Jagrat: *awaken*

Jal: *water*

Jatharagni: *fire of digestion*

Jnana Mudra: *a specific mudra or gesture of hands used in sadhana indicating knowledge*

Jnana: *knowledge*

Jnanakanda: *knowledge aspect of religion*

Jyotish: *study of grahas for predictive purposes*

Kailasa: *abode of Shiva*

Kala: *time*

Kalaratri: *a dark night; also name of a goddess*

Kalasamkarsini: *a form of Kali*

Kalikula: *one school of Tantra that worships Kali and related deities*

Kama: *lust or desire*

Kamadeva: *God of desire and lust*

Kamakhya: *Mahamaya goddess of Kamakhya*

Kankala Murti: *one form of Shiva like a skeleton*

Kapalamochana: *name of a place in Kashi*

Kapalika: *an extreme form of upasaka*

Karmakanda: *ritual aspect of religion*

Karotaka: *name of a great Naga*

Kartikeya: *a deity who is the son of Shiva and Parvati*

Kathamrita: *biography of Sri Ramakrishna*

Kathasaritsagara: *a famous eleventh century collection of Indian stories*

Kaula: *one initiated into tantric upasana*

Kaulachara: *Kaula mode of worship*

Kenopanishad: *one of the Upanishads*

Khadga: *sword of large sacrificial knife*

Khatvanga: *the weapon held by the form of Bhairava and Devi*

Khechari: *a kind of yogic process and siddhi that allows a person to fly*

Kilana: *a spiritual circle for protection*

Kosha: *one of the five sheaths that cover a human being*

Krama: *stages of sadhana*

Krishna: *Yadava hero and avatar of Vishnu*

Kriya: *a kind of yoga*

Kshetra: *holy place*

Kshetrajna: *knower of the field or kshetra*

Kubjika: *a form of Goddess*

Kula Devata: *family deity*

Kulamarga: *path of kula*

Kulavriksha: *the tree linked to a kula*

Kundalini: *secret hidden power inside the human body*

Lagna: *an imaginary point in the birth horoscope from where analysis begins*

Lagnashuddhi: *purification of the body*

Lingam: *an iconic form of Shiva*

Madhava: *founder of the Dvaita school of Vedanta*

Madhuchchhandas: *name of a rishi*

Madya: *alcohol*

Maha Bhairavi: *great bhairavi*

Mahakarshana: *great attraction*

Mahamurkha: *fool*

Mahanirvana Tantra: *a tantric text*

Mahapandita: *great scholar*

Mahapralaya: *great deluge at end of creation*

Mahapreta: *great preta*

Mahashakti: *great goddess*

Mahashivaratri: *great night of Lord Shiva*

Mahavidya: *great wisdom goddess*

Mahavira: *great hero*

Mahavrata: *great penance performed for Bhairava*

Mahavratin: *one who follows the mahavrata*

Mahayana: *greater vehicle; a path in Buddhism*

Mahi: *Vedic goddess*

Mahishasura: *a buffalo asura who was killed by Durga*

Maithuna: *sex*

Mamsa: *meat*

Manas: *mind*

Manava Grihyasutra: *a ritual text containing directions for domestic ceremonies*

Mandala: *a yantric diagram or a period of sadhana*

Manipura: *the chakra at the solar plexus*

Manolaya: *end of normal mind*

Manomaya Kosha: *mental shealth*

Manonasha: *transcending the normal mind*

Mantra Japa: *chanting of mantra*

Marg: *path*

Matrika: *spiritual feminine deities that surround the primary deity*

Matsya: *fish*

Matsyendra: *a great Nath yogi from ancient India*

Mayavivarta: *a theory on world appearance and Brahma used in Advaita Vedanta*

Mimamsaka: *critical investigation, also a school of studying Vedas*

Mitra: *Vedic god*

Moksha: *liberation*

Mooladhara: *first chakra in the human body*

Moolmantra: *primary mantra*

Mudgala Purana: *one scripture dealing with Ganpati upasana*

Mudra: *parched grains*

Mukti: *liberation*

Mundasana: *a seat made of skulls*

Murti: *idol*

Naga Sadhu: *a kind of sanyasi*

Naga: *great snakes*

Namaskara: *bowing*

Nara: *human being*

Narasimha: *man-lion incarnation of Vishnu*

Natha Yogi: *a band of legendary itinerant yogis*

Nati: *a dancer*

Nilachala: *blue mountains*

Nilakantha: *blue-throated*

Nimittamatra: *a mere instrument*

Ninya Vacamsi: *secret words*

Niradhara: *without an adhara of support*

Niyama: *rules often self-imposed*

Nyasa: *placement of sacred syllables on the body*

Ojas: *vigour and vitality*

Padma: lotus

Padmasana: yogic posture

Pancatattwa: five elements used in Shakti upasana

Panchamukha Hanuman: Hanuman with five faces

Para: the highest Shakti

Parameshwara: great God

Parampara: tradition

Paravak: the highest form of speech

Parijata: a flower

Pasa: chains that bind consciousness

Paschimamnaya: Western school of transmission of Tantra

Pashu: animal

Pashupata: a sect of Saivas

Patala Bhairavi: a bhairavi form who resides in patala, the Hell or the lowest realms

Pavaka: pure

Pingla: subtle channel in the right side of the body

Pitha: special place of divine power

Pitr Yajna: ritual to placate ancestors

Pitr: ancestors

Pitta: one of the type of physical disposition used in ayurveda, identified with fire

Prachanda Chandika: another name of Chinnamasta

Prakriti: nature

Pramanavada: knowledge and study of cognition

Prana Shakti: life force

Pranamaya Kosha: one of the sheaths covering the human body made of life force

Pranapratishthapana: establishing prana or life force in a murti

Pratyalidha: posture of standing

Prayoga: *application*

Preta: *one type of spirit which is malevolent*

Prithvi: *earth*

Purusha: *male principle*

Purva Samskaras: *tendencies from past births*

Rahu: *a graha, one of lunar nodes*

Raja Yoga: *a path of spiritual growth*

Rajas: *guna of activity*

Rakshasa: *malefic entity*

Raktashuddhi: *purification of blood*

Rama: *avatar of Vishnu*

Ramayana: *Hindu epic that describes the story of Lord Rama*

Rati: *the consort of Kamadeva*

Ravana: *the rakshasa whom Rama defeated in battle*

Rik: *a specific type of composition most commonly found in the Rig Veda*

Ripus: *internal enemies of any individual like lust, greed, anger, etc.*

Rishi: *spiritual seers*

Rtam: *the divine law that governs Truth*

Rudra: *Vedic god*

Sabar Tantra: *non-Sanskrit Tantra*

Sadhaka: *spiritual practitioner*

Sadhana: *process of spiritual practice*

Sadhanakrama: *stage of sadhana*

Sadhanamala: *a tantric text*

Sahasradala: *a thousand-petalled lotus*

Sahasrara: *a thousand-petalled lotus overhead*

Sakshi bhava: *remaning as a witness*

Samadhi: *absorption in yoga or meditation*

Samaj: *community*

Samata: *equipoise*

Samkhya: *one philosophy of Hinduism*

Sampradaya: *sect within Hinduism*

Samsara: *world*

Sanatana Dharma: *the Hindu religion*

Sandhi: *period of change between two times*

Sandhya Bhasha: *twilight language*

Saraswati: *goddess of artistic inspirations and knowledge*

Sarpasatra: *yajna to destroy snakes*

Sarvabuddhadakini: *name of Chinnamasta*

Sarvasiddhi: *all siddhis*

Sasana: *rule*

Satchidananda: *truth force bliss attributes of the Brahma*

Satguru: *a supreme guide or master*

Satsang: *spiritual company*

Sattva: *guna of lightness*

Shakta: *pertaining to Shakti*

Shakti: *power*

Shaktipitha: *kshetra of Shakti*

Shankha: *conch*

Shastra: *scriptures*

Shastric: *pertaining to shastra*

Shava: *dead body*

Shesha Naga: *the Naga who holds the earth on his hood*

Shishya: *disciple*

Shiva: *Hindu god*

Shuddhacinacararata: *engaged in pure cinacara*

Siddha: *accomplished soul*

Siddhi: *special accomplishment in the spiritual path*

Sivasimhasanasthitam: *a throne of Shiva on which Devi is seated*

Skanda: *Hindu devata*

Smashana: *cremation ground*

Somasiddhantin: *follower of one extreme sect of Saivism*

Sri Rama: *avatar of Vishnu*

Srikula: *one school of Tantra that worships Lalita Tripurasundari*

Srimad Bhagwatam: *a Vaishnava scripture*

Stotra: *a hymn of praise*

Sukha: *bliss*

Sukhasana: *yogic posture*

Sushumna: *central spiritual channel*

Sushupti: *deep dreamless sleep*

Svah: *mental realm*

Swadharma: *one's Dharma*

Swapna: *dreams*

Swara: *breathing*

Takshaka: *a Naga*

Tamas: *guna of dullness*

Tandava Nritya: *dance of Shiva*

Tantra: *method of upasana*

Tantrasara: *a compendium of tantric upasanas*

Tantrika: *one who practices Tantra upasana*

Tantropasaka: *one who does Tantra sadhana*

Tapas: *spiritual penance*

Tattva: *attribute*

Tattvashuddhi: *purification of tattvas*

Tatwvavichara: *understanding of attributes*

Tejas: *effulgence*

Tithi: *angular distance between sun and moon used in Hindu calendar*

Treta Yuga: *one yuga or cycle of time*

Triguna: *three gunas*

Tripura Bhairavi: *a Mahavidya devi*

Tripurasundari Sodasi: *a Mahavidya goddess, attaining whom is the aim of all Srividya upasana*

Trishula: *trident of Shiva*

Turiyam: *the fourth state of consciousness*

Ucchista Ganpati: *a form of Ganpati*

Ugra: *fierce*

Upadesam: *advice on mantra*

Upanishad: *religious texts*

Upasaka: *one who does worship of gods*

Upasana: *worship of devatas*

Uttaramnaya: *school of northern transmission*

Uttarasadhaka: *advanced sadhaka*

Vahana: *vehicle*

Vaishnavism: *worship of Vishnu*

Vajra: *thunderbolt*

Vajravairochani: *a goddess in Tibetan Buddhism*

Vajravarahi: *a form of varahi prayed in Buddhism*

Vakra: *curved*

Vakreshwari: *a form of goddess*

Vaksiddhi: *perfection in speech*

Vamachara: *left hand path of Tantra*

Vamadeva: *one of the rishis*

Vanara: *monkey*

Varada Mudra: *gesture of fingers used to indicate blessings*

Varaha: *a boar incarnation of Vishnu*

Vashistha: *rishi*

Vasuki: *the Naga who lies coiled in the throat of Lord Shiva*

Vatuka: *Bhairava in the form of a small child*

Vayu: *air*

Vedachara: *Vedic mode of worship*

Vedanga: *fields of study needed for learning the Vedas*

Vedanta: *one school of Hindu philosophy*

Vedavadaviruddha: *opposed to Vedas*

Vedic Samhita: *core text of the Vedas*

Vibhuti: *sacred ash*

Vidya: *knowledge*

Vigraha: *murti of a god or goddess*

Vinayaka: *one name of Ganpati*

Vira: *brave or hero, a category of upasaka*

Virabhava: *attitude of vira*

Virodha Bhakti: *devotion through opposition*

Vishada: *despondency*

Vishnukranta: *a geographical area where a specific type of Tantra was prevalent*

Vishwarupa: *universal form*

Viveka: *inner power of discrimination*

Vritahan: *an asura killed by Indra*

Vasanta Panchami: *a day of worshipping Devi Saraswati*

Yagyopavita: *sacred thread*

Yajna: *sacrifical ritual aimed to propitiate gods*

Yajnavalkya Smriti: *a Dharma related text of Hinduism*

Yaksha: *another class of ethereal beings*

Yamala: *union*

Yantra: *mystical diagram*

Yogi: *one who practices yoga*
Yogini: *advanced spiritual female being*
Yoni Puja: *worship of womb*
Yonigahvara: *cave of the womb*
Yuga: *a phase of time*

Books by BluOne Ink

Kali Imprint

Sri Aurobindo & the Literary Renaissance of India | Pariksith Singh
ISBN: 9788194954781 | ₹995

Sri Aurobindo and Philosophy | Pariksith Singh
ISBN: 9789392209017 | ₹995

Somewhere Among the Stars | Adi Varuni
ISBN: 9789392209215 | ₹395

The Eternal Feminine | Dr. Alok Pandey
ISBN: 9788194954774 | ₹699

Integral Education | Partho
ISBN: 9788194954705 | ₹499

Hindutva: Origin, Evolution and Future | Aravindan Neelakandan
ISBN: 9789392209062 | ₹995

Symbols and Parables | Dr Alok Pandey
ISBN: 9789392209376 | ₹295

BluPrint Imprint

Identity's Last Secret | Makarand R Paranjape
ISBN: 9788194954798 | ₹1495

Swayam Se Parichay (in Hindi) | Pariksith Singh
ISBN: 9789392209185 | ₹195

Chhutti Ke Din (bilingual in Hindi and Rajasthani) | Pariksith Singh
ISBN: 9789392209024 | ₹699

Anjali Geetan Ri (in Rajasthani) | Ikraam Rajasthani
ISBN: 9789392209277 | ₹250

Jana Awjanar Majhe (in Bengali) | Bimal Chakravartty
ISBN: 9789392209277 | ₹250

The Eternal Gene and Other Tales of Malaise | Ankush Sam Thorpe
ISBN: 9789392209147 | ₹495

Swayam ka Ghuspaithiya | Pariksith Singh
ISBN: 9789392209192 | ₹699

Occam Imprint

Confidence Cures | Lt Gen. S. B. Sehajpal and Mrs Kiran Sehajpal
ISBN: 9789392209260 | ₹495

War Despatches 1971 | Brig. B. S. Mehta
ISBN: 9789392209123 | ₹899

March to Justice | Navdeep Singh and Frank Rosenblatt
ISBN: 9788194954712 | ₹995

The Fighting Fourth | Brig. Jasbir Singh, SM,
ISBN: 9788194954750 | ₹699

Once Upon a Time in RIMC | Brig. Jasbir Singh, SM
ISBN: 9788194954729 | ₹250

Design: A Business Case | Brigitte Borja de Mozota and
Steinar Valade-Amland
ISBN: 9788194954743 | ₹795

MRA Made Simple: Seriously? | Pariksith Singh, MD and
Lynda Dilts-Benson
ISBN: 9781954261006 | $29.99

Compliance Made Simple: Seriously? | Pariksith Singh, MD and
Lynda Dilts-Benson
ISBN: 9781954261013 | $55.99

Snakes in the Ganga: Breaking India 2.0 | Rajiv Malhotra and
Vijaya Viswanathan
ISBN: 9789392209093 | ₹895

Life of an Industani: Six Degrees of Separation | Shiv Kunal Verma
ISBN: 9789392209154 | ₹995

Bharat ke Janjatiya Krantiveer: Swatantrata Sangram ki 75 Unsuni Kahaniyaan (in Hindi) | Dhaval Patel
ISBN: 9789392209161 | ₹695

Grit to Glory | Brig. B.S. Mehta
ISBN: 9789392209291 | ₹895

The Battle for IITs: A Defense of Meritocracy | Rajiv Malhotra and Vijaya Viswanathan
ISBN: 9789392209314 | ₹250

Varna, Jati, Caste: A Primer on Indian Social Structures | Rajiv Malhotra and Vijaya Viswanathan
ISBN: 9789392209345 | ₹250

The Power of Future Machines: Essays on Artificial Intelligence | Rajiv Malhotra, T.N. Sudarshan and Manogna Sastry (Eds)
ISBN: 9789392209338 | ₹750

Of Newtons and Apples: Insights into 50 Great Minds in Human History | Dr Abhishek Kumar
ISBN: 9789392209246 | ₹350

Our Forthcoming Titles

Seeing with Hands | Jinan K.B.
ISBN: 9789392209420

The Quest: An artist's journey within | Aparajita
ISBN: 9789392209437

Purvyam: Before the Beginning | Abhishek Talwar
ISBN: 9789392209413

Construction Industry 2.0 | Akhilesh Srivastava
ISBN: 9789392209352

Sobha Singh Artist: Life and Legacy | Dr Hirday Paul Singh
ISBN: 9789392209369

Probashir Golpo Shongroho | Bimal Chakravartty
ISBN: 9789392209383